Thrills and Chills:

Demagoguery, Charisma and Freedom with Max Weber,

Emile Durkheim & J.J. Rousseau

by Roy Berger

Photos copyright by Roy Berger

Faux-Pas Press

Ottawa

Canada

Copyright 2016

theprinceofcornwall@yahoo.com

First Edition

Library and Archives Canada Cataloguing

English Print Edition

ISBN# 978-0-9877363-7-6

English Electronic Edition

ISBN# 978-0-9877363-8-3

French Print Edition

ISBN# 978-0-9877363-9-0

French Electronic Edition

ISBN# 978-0-9958159-0-2

g

Introduction

Chairs and thrones await our philosopher Kings. It is suggested that they walk among us. Those chairs of influence have yet to be filled and not been filled in post-modern memory. Accompanied by the unseen hand we are left to our own devices half blundering our way to tomorrow, attempting to make sense of yesterday. Fortunately, there are vast tracks in the snow to follow. We have been preceded by great and unclouded minds who truly pursued truths and social conditions.

Critical understanding remains a useful tool in handling the flow of information; its interactive qualities not withstanding and like a determined cloud the Constitutional Proposals never really vanished and exist as a departure point for discussion and remain an exciting read.

In these three tasty, essay, info-snacks I have not been guilty of being unbiased. Good science is it's own bias and is applicable over time and space like a math formula that can be duplicated regardless of region or time of day to produce the same answer. Coming to an understanding about the mechanics of a social group is as valuable as having the combination to a vault. Our history is a daily scientific precipice.

Many forms of the internet were in their infancy at the original time of writing however I found it necessarily desirable to touch base with it here and there lest, you think I'm too prescient.

There's a time to run, a time to duck and a time to plan. If you're reading this, it's proof your ancestors did all those things at the appropriate times.

Methods of distributing the propaganda evolve. Who can provide ink, paper and a printing press? Who can provide the electricity to operate the internet? Who cares about solar coronal mass ejections? All the social actors in society do not receive the same information at the same rate, nor is the information processed in the same way. Who has the encryption key, password and memory card?

The works of these masters translate well over time and space. They remain vital and their foundations matter. As I unearth these works I'm convinced they matter still and more than yesterday because we are here now.

Group dynamic theory will support that as groups develop there will be disparity of thought, opinion and ultimately distribution of power. And power is a very big deal indeed. Whether power is legitimate, rational or even legal – we do know it's a bag of wet angry determined cats. Here's my bag of angry cats. Don't forget to duck and cover.

Just prior to publishing I received a telegram from Max Weber. He writes that he is in the process of formatting three new books: *The Artificial Intelligence Ethic and the Spirit of Capitalism, Robotic Economy and Society* and what he figured would be his biggest hit, *Surveillance as A Vocation*. I know we can look forward to his influence for some time.

Thank you, sincerely, Roy Berger.

Table of Contents

This is where I go on an on about well, demagogues, leaders and those that would challenge them. Oh yeah, and the power that comes from sticks and stones and the words that crush you forever.

The first few times I read the Canadian Constitutional Proposals I knew I'd have to tell everyone about it. Rousseau is so hip and cool that I think if he had his own website he'd probably be using Janis Joplin and Bob Dylan sound-tracks in the background. He's our granddaddy of democracy.

Weber lets it all hang out when we get to know the charismatic and how that's different from just being popular on payday. When we get excited and go on the march or if we want to get our neighbours excited and go on the march we must look into our feel better hearts while Buddy 'the charismatic one', pulls off a couple of miracles.

Domination by Spinmasters from the Planet Earth:

From Under the Boot to Resistance

Life without domination would be life in perfect balance. This ideal (type) world would be without conflict, without change and would be stagnant and without challenge. Evolution would have effectively stopped. However, domination is alive, well and around us all the time. It is holding our belief patterns in check and guiding our values and spirits. Sometimes it tries to shake up existing values and replace them with others.

Domination as an ideal-type concept exists without value. It is neither positive nor negative, it is just the name we give a force, one that is different from 'power'. Domination is different from power in that domination offers punishment for the rule-breaker who would go against the tide. Domination contains coercion, either implied, imagined, or real. Domination can take the form of a paradigm vigorously defended by a group of scientists who have the power to recommend grants[1] and loans for research programs or it can take the form of strapping the hands of a young child caught chewing gum in class.

Domination, too, can offer great rewards, as may be used in certain cults. Follow these lessons carefully, give

---

[1] See Thomas Kuhn, *The Structure of Scientific Revolution*

all of yourself to *Bob*. Think only of Bob and you will go to *'Slack Heaven'*. In time and by the use of certain tools of domination, you are soon dominated by *'The Church of Bob'* with its promises, rationalizations and dogmatic mottos, surprising yourself by selling pencils in airports for The Church of Bob.

Domination as a Course of Social Action

"The social relationship thus consists entirely and exclusively in the existence of a probability that there will be, in some meaningfully understandable sense, a course of social action." [2]

The Definition, meaning and criteria for a social relationship matches that which is necessary to allow the formation of domination. They both require that which is necessary to allow the formation of domination. They both require mutual consent, deliberation and social action. They are both an agreement, a common decision and they can vary, like so much else, in intensity, frequency and duration.

As Weber writes this selection he is, of course, only capable of defining the terms and does not provide a mathematical statement of probability of a social relationship. Also, we can't say that "domination" and "social relationship" are the same thing but we can not safely say that one can happen without the other. That is, if there is domination there must be a social relationship,

---

[2] J.E.T. Eldridge, ed. *Max Weber: The Interpretation of Social Reality*. (London, Joseph, 1970), page 91.

but if there is a social relationship it doesn't presuppose domination. Domination implies an imbalance of power. But an imbalance of power doesn't presuppose conflict.

Social relationships, Weber argues, "…may be influenced by the creation of differential advantages which favour one type over another." Everything else in may effect these differential advantages, that is, "All changes of natural social conditions have some sort of effect on the differential probabilities of survival of social relationships." [3]

So the limitation of prediction here, from an empirical view, is availability of data, identification of the relevant indicators and a system of correlation of the data, indicators and social relationships. Solving this would be a significant step towards predicting domination within a probability that could be dealt with in an interval ratio level of measurement. One function of bureaucracy is to collect data and create systems.

Organized Domination – Bureaucracy

"Discipline and its sister, bureaucracy, presuppose an allegiance to one other than the self; an institution, state, bosses. It assumes domination by virtue of a subtle or obvious deindividuation. To observe bureaucracy is to believe in something else other than family, community, or friendship as that to appease, obey and conform to."[4]

---

[3] Ibid. page 86.
[4] *Max Weber. Economy and Society: An Outline of Interpretive Sociology.* Ed. Guenther

Weber recognized that "organized domination"[5], or order, since it is so closely linked to the legitimate use of violence, demands a continuous administration or bureaucracy to enforce it. Bureaucracy is necessary for "organized domination". Here Weber's consideration on the university proves useful:

"Lacking a sense of civil self-esteem and a sense of responsibility for their own actions, the German people showed no inclination, or capacity to maintain their independence in the face of political leaders of charismatic genius and a powerful bureaucracy." [6]

In the original context of this quote from the introduction, E. Shils is referring to the rise of Otto Von Bismarck in Germany and its impact on the German population's civility. This is indeed a mix of all three of Weber's pure types of domination. Bismarck's legacy of legal, traditional and charismatic domination squeezed out civility and slowly replaced it with acquiescence. There was no torture, taxes or angry killer bees and the fate of German intellectualism was sealed thirteen years later in the eager bowing and scraping before Adolph Hitler.

Roth & Claus Wittich (New York, Bedminster Press, 1968) page 1149.

[5] H.H. Gerth & C. Wright Mills, eds & trans. *From Max Weber* (London, Routledge & Kegan Paul, 1970) page 80.

[6] *Max Weber on Universities*. Ed & trans. Edward Shils (Chicago, University of Chicago Press, 1974) page 3.

Domination and Legitimacy

While Weber is quick to point out that domination does not overtly always use wealth as a means for maintaining itself it does have a more indirect method: "...this is just what happens in one way or another and often to such an extent that the mode of applying economic means for the purpose of maintaining domination, in turn, exercises a determining influence on the structure of domination."[7]

It may be that the contest between legitimacy and domination is exercised in the current back and forth drama between marijuana dispensaries and the law where the dispensaries are paying taxes to the government shutting them down. Both parties claim rational legitimacy.

"Both in notable and bureaucratic administrations the structure of state power has influenced culture very strongly...from justice to education...demands on culture, in turn, are determined, through to a varying extent, by the growing wealth of the most influential strata in the state." [8]

Another example is the impact of raising university student tuition fees in times of economic recession or doing away with or lowering grant schemes. The indirect result of this is that differential access to higher education

---

[7] Max Weber. *Economy and Society*, page 942

[8] Gerth & Mills. *From Max Weber*, page 212.

is created, thus preventing more of the underclass from achieving intellectual domination than the more economically privileged. This helps to maintain a particular status quo in times when it may well be argued that an underclass more familiar with the impact of financial constraint on humanity might be better able to deal with social problems. Due to their proximity and familiarity, the underclass, as opposed to those in the ivory tower, are in a better position to problem-solve. This reaffirms Rousseau's assertion that humans have the ability to create environments contrary to their best interest.

The structure of domination then is seen as the traditional means of producing the intellectual elite.

Monopoly of Goods and services can lead to

<Domination>

Can lead to authority, command and duty.

One can lead to the other. A monopoly on guns, drugs or gold or a monopoly on authority, command and duty can lead to domination. Think of Colonel Oliver North, the Contras, cocaine, Ronald Reagan and a war not approved of by the Senate. Things of the market place can place its purveyor in a dominant position of authority. Others may follow orders out of self-interest or self-survival. We see this in both the Golden Triangle of Thailand and the cocaine cartels of South America. In both cases, the drug monopoly has led to direct involvement of drug lords in legitimate and illegitimate authority in relation to the government, its subjects, the military and the sphere of foreign neighbours.

Domination is defined by Weber as **"The command of the ruler will be obeyed, for its own sake, by the ruled."** [9] This is empathy, inspiration, persuasion or some combination of valid norms.

Domination in Suspension

This is that peculiar point in time where there are sanctions, punishment, orders and activity, but its source is non-specific. No one knows who the boss is, yet the by-product is that by standing employees or citizens feel the punishment of sanctions, even if inadvertent. An example of this would be the surprise freezing of a company's bank account. Paycheques for employees and creditors would bounce. Accounts and credit ratings could be affected. Unsecured creditors are painfully surprised. At a moment like this it's hard to know who is boss or how to make the cheques good, yet pain is felt. The 2016 Phoenix payroll program utilized in Ottawa had problems resulting in almost 80,000 public service employees having their paycheques interrupted. Thousands had not been paid in months. Financial pain and anxiety was felt by social

[9] Op. cit., page 946

actors even though it was unintended and there didn't appear to be a single villain but rather a misunderstood computer program.

Another example of domination in suspension could be a pattern of mysterious theft. In mid-October 1992 the New Democratic Party Montreal headquarters had their office broken into and had their computer hard-drive stolen. Hard-drives tend to contain files and lists. Later, in December 4th, 1992 the Simone de Beauvoir Institute at Concordia University had a similar theft, as well as its Campus Ministry and First Nations Concordia. Three days later, the same thing happened to the hard-drive share by the Concordia University Student's Association Employee's Union at the CUSA job bank in the Hall building. (All in Montreal.) All these groups fit a pattern in that they may be labeled slightly left in their politics. Regardless of the motive, the source of dominating activity is unknown and a population segment is punished.

The Dissolving of Overt Domination in a Democracy with Many Industrial Concerns

Movement towards balance may be said to be a lessening of domination with reference to a general or specific social relationship. There are two significant and clear examples of this intent in the most recent *Beaudoin/Dobbie Canadian Constitutional Proposals:*

The Report of the Special Joint Committee on a Renewed Canada. Sen Beaudoin, Dobbie M.P., February 28, 1992 Canada Communications Group:

"We recommend;

1) **In order to protect the aboriginal and treaty rights which the Constitution guarantees to the aboriginal peoples of Canada, that any amendment to the Constitution of Canada directly affecting the aboriginal peoples require the consent of the aboriginal peoples of Canada prior to its implementation;**
2) **That representatives of the aboriginal peoples of Canada be invited to all future constitutional conferences relating to the matters refereed to in paragraph 1."** [10]

The intent or proposal (legal-rational) is to move from the domineering heavy-handed Indian Act of 1867, which derogates and restricts native participation in life and law to one which requires their representation for Canadian life and law to work. The domination of Canadian law is not removed but, some would argue, the sting would be removed by mutual consent.

A second example of the lessening of dissolution of domination is the inclusion of The Right to Privacy, which did not exist in the previous recommendation. **"In a society in which surveillance has increased, the right to privacy will become even more important."** [11]

---

[10] *Constitutional Proposals*, Beaudoin Report, p. 32
[11] Ibid., p. 37

The reduction of domination by legal lawful instruments can be accomplished through mutual consent and is in no way an example of passive acquiescence as the issue is dealt with in an overt manner.

This then brings us to a discussion of the reduction of domination by illegal lawful instruments. I would say that guerrilla warfare, peasant uprisings and the resistance of indigenous populations to imperialism is lawful when it has as its goal the reduction of repression and carries with it the popular support or blessing of the masses.

I'm going to place whistle blowing and leaking here as a form of illegal behavior and where it seeks to attack a dominant legal rational group, be seen as a form of guerilla behavior. Edward Snowden and Julian Assange fit this characteristic of post-modern guerrillas using leaks and USB's as weapons.

"The more secretive or unjust an organization is, the more leaks induce fear and paranoia in its leadership and planning coterie. This must result in minimization of efficient internal communications mechanisms (an increase in cognitive "secrecy tax") and consequent system-wide cognitive decline resulting in decreased ability to hold onto power as the environment demands adaption.

Hence in a world where leaking is easy, secretive or unjust systems are nonlinearly hit relative to open, just systems. Since unjust systems, by their nature induce opponents, and in many places barely have the upper hand, mass leaking leaves them exquisitely vulnerable to those who seek to replace them with more open forms of governance." [12]

Terrorism, on the other hand, is an unlawful instrument because of its contention that the masses will be held accountable for the repression and therefore becomes a target.

Psychic Coercion & Terrorism as a Form of and Reaction to Domination

Terrorism, as naked aggression against an unwitting populace, is a form of coercion. Coercion in this instance, although brutal and physical in form, manifests itself psychically in actuality. Its intent is to change the predominant belief system, by way of rational exploitation of the citizenry into one more palatable to

---

[12] Julian Assange, Sun 31 Dec 2006: *The non linear effects of leaks on unjust systems of governance*. Web archive.

the insurgent army. Terrorism is a particular form of coercion which lives in the breath of new paradigms seeking to burst the anomic bubble.

Guerrilla warfare, be it urban or rural, and terrorism can seek the reduction of domination through the use of illegal instruments and is often in direct opposition to the state as the sole bearer of the "legitimate use of violence".

Tools of Domination

In Weber's remarks on *"Democratization and Demagoguery"* [13], he makes several assertions that are important to both the sociological tools of domination and the cleansing process that can be a part of demagoguery.

---

[13] 11 Max Weber, *Economy and Society*, p. 1450

Firstly, Weber illustrates that promotion of an actor from subordinate to superordinate will often be accompanied by "profound skepticism" in relation to the motives and means of the promoted one. Secondly, he points out that a rise to public power, certainly within the political arena, may bring with it exposure "**...to public scrutiny through the criticism of opponents and competitors**" [14]

[Note of caution: Where there is a connection between exposure, the exposed and the ownership of the means of producing exposure the reader must maintain an element of skepticism.]

This struggle, this political domination for particular interests, Weber feels can generally be "**accomplished better by the much maligned 'craft of demagoguery' than by the clerk's office...**" [15], and demagoguery can seek to dominate through tools: "**They use speeches, telegrams, and propaganda devices of all kinds for the promotion of their prestige; nobody can claim that this kind of political propaganda has proved less dangerous for the national interest than the most passionate demagogy at election time.**" [16]

Awareness of domination is not required and is generally supressed or manipulated in the spirit of false consciousness. This is *The Shadow's* cloak of domination with the power to cloud the minds of men.

---

[14] Ibid
[15] Ibid.
[16] Ibid., p. 1451

Censorship: A Tool of Domination

"The king controls speech as well as action. War is always accompanied by censorship, and people are most easily controlled in isolation. The Censor keeps us from reaching out, from making connections." [17]

Censorship is alive right here at home. Witness the Dec. 6th, 1992 publication ban of the CBC's, Boys of St. Vincent with holding showings in Montreal and Ontario only to allow its distribution the following week.

Censorship in regards to thought and speech is certainly as old as the liberty it tends to constrain. The Foreign Intelligence column of The London Chronicle reveals a lovely example of severe censorship:

"The National Assembly having sent into Germany many members of the congregation of what is called the Propaganda, to disseminate democratic principles there, principles which cannot assimilate with the constitution of the empire, a rigorous law shall be enacted, ordaining that every Frenchman or German who shall profess these principles either in public or private, shall be punished with death." [18]

---

[17] 15 Starhawk. *Truth or Dare: Encounters With Power, Authority, and Mastery* (San Francisco, Harper & Row, 1990), p. 177

[18] *The London Chronicle*, July 5-7, 1791, p. 17

So censorship can be seemingly trivial or heavy-handed. Loose censorship can allow a war journalist to roam freely as in the Vietnam war or contrary wise have their movements more controlled by being embedded with the home troops.

Failure to censor or refusal to censor can bring reprisal consisting of fines, jail term, loss of printing license perhaps, or a legal threat of libel for any national publication daring to print uncomfortable words. Failure to censor may also bring about defeat. Secret plans of wars and lovers are occasionally upset by loose lips and the unintended discovery of documents that censorship would have prevented.

Failure to censor dinner conversation - self-censorship. It was a common rule of thumb that one did not discuss sex, religion or politics unless one was willing to confront the sanctions or threat of sanctions such as early departure, expulsion, dirty looks or failure in the future to make the 'A' party list. This is domination of a prevailing social current or wind supported by school, church, employer, media, ourselves and a plethora of social nuances that prevent the citizen from self-examination by exploring social, political and religious ideas which are part of the foundations of sociology.

Knowledge can become power that resists domination. So the domination of one belief or ideology can struggle towards the goal of ignorance or false consciousness by using the tool of censorship. Ideal knowledge will struggle to limit censorship. Then so can the leaking of information be a tool that resists domination?

The goal of misinformation, ignorance and maintenance of false consciousness for the purpose of domination is admirably demonstrated by the 1992 decision of the International War Crimes Tribunal.

This New York based tribunal, using as reference law treaties, the Geneva Convention, the Nuremberg trials and the United Nations Charter, found President George Bush guilty of war crimes. Will the U.N. Global Cops move on this one?

This significant story, however, was not covered in the American media even though or perhaps because: **"This is the first time a tribunal has charged the military victors with war crimes while it is still in power..."** [19]

Negative moral or ethical implications of a recent war or erosion of faith in a national leader could have negative consequences for the domination of the state, in that there is a threat to a current fostered belief and hard-core fence sitting. Therefore, downsizing, downplaying, generating confidence, or providing a

---

[19] *The Montreal Mirror*, March 26, 1992

"news black out" would serve the status quo best by maintaining the ignorance of the masses.

The was also tried by Hydro-Quebec in an attempt to suppress aluminium smelter contracts by getting a gag order to constrain the watchful eyes of the Canadian press. This backfired as the media was coerced into obeying the order and the public was influenced in the direction of anti-Hydro Quebec and anti-state feelings by the "secret deal" between public and private concerns complicated by the use of the court. The "secret deal" would eventually come to light by the Australian press.

Thomas Mann speaks of the goal of education under the Nazis:

"The result is that education is never for its own sake; its content is never confined to training, culture, knowledge, the furtherance of human progress through instruction. Instead it had sole reference, often enough with violent implications, to the fixed idea of national pre-eminence and warlike preparedness." [20]

"Human beings – the Germans proved this during the war – can become accustomed to almost anything if they are led to believe its necessity." [21]

---

[20] Erika Mann. *School for Barbarians: Education Under the Nazis* (London, Lindsay Drummond Ltd., 1939) p. IX

[21] Ibid., p. 29

This 'conquest of the inner enemy' that Mann aptly describes is well-documented elsewhere and is done through physical and psychological coercion coupled with the desire to obey for its own rewards and the threat of sanctions for disobeying.

Erika Mann asserts: **"The German Republic refused to influence its citizens one way or the other, or to convince them of the advantages of demagoguery; it did not carry on anti-propaganda in its own favor."** [22] This may have been an example of the "ethical neutrality" that Weber spoke of in 1917 in *'The Academic Calling in Imperial Germany'* where he argues, if I'm reading between the lines correctly, that there are those who would oppose the university from taking a political stand on the grounds of ethical neutrality. These opponents believe that a political stance would discredit cultural and social discussion which take place both in an away from the university lecture hall.[23]

In *'Science as a Vocation'* Weber warns of bringing politics into the classroom. There is no contradiction here between Weber and my own polemic. The difference between politics in the classroom and the University as a whole engaging in the public debate on crucial issues is just that...public. This is akin to the public and private personal and are of declaration. If the

[22] Ibid., p. 37
[23] *Max Weber on Universities*, p. 51

University enters into outside debate it is subject to the inquiry, skepticism and flurry that steers all the other players and social actors. This is apart from and not in conflict with the inquiry that takes place in the private lecture hall or classroom where rationality is explored and defined with various degrees of certainty and clarity. Direction is the key here.

The University can challenge the city and the professor can challenge the student. The problem is also this: can the reverse be possible and what has happened to either sets of circumstances? Dr. Timothy Leary challenged Harvard (the establishment) in the early 1960's and was shamed and disgraced. In the summer of 1992 Claude Morin admitted that he was an informant (code name - French Minuet) aiding the RCMP by turning in the names of left-leaning students during the 1950's and 1960's while a professor at the University of Laval. No professor in Canada dared to publicly criticize that behavior.

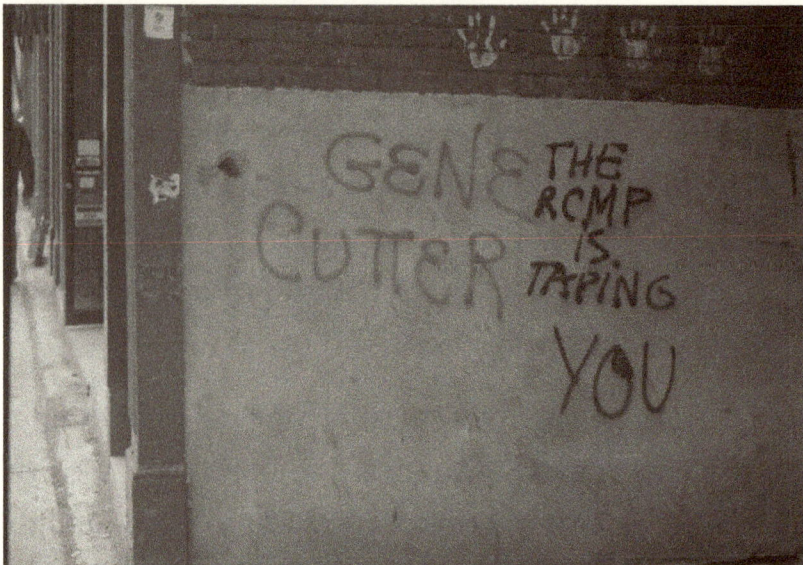

"...Max Weber's view that the university teacher must, if he wishes to express his views about authority and the policies it should follow, take the responsibility for doing so on himself and not allow it to appear that is unquestionably 'given' by the 'facts' and hence lies outside his own moral responsibility." [24]

I think the essence here is that one should not abdicate one's authority for the self, morality or education to others. One must be aware of the peculiar phenomenon of the role of the state and the university in the quest for truth and knowledge, especially if that knowledge prescribes venturing down a particular avenue of questioning or action. Herein lies a particular domination game where few are privy and little is written.

---

[24] Ibid., p. 2

One would have to be blind as a bat not to understand that by 1991, "Post-Oka"[25] Canada was in a state of economic and constitutional crises, coupled with an unpopular government and the threat of Quebec separation. For want of a better term, it's a mess and we must look at what tools, institutions, beliefs and ideologies are at hand to reduce the strain and conflict. We must then make choices and not reduce ourselves to upholding *Robert's Rules of Order* the way another generation held up Chairman Mao's 'little red book'. One procedure orientated with no content, the other, all content with no procedure.

---

[25] See *Kanehsatake 270 Years of Resistance*, Alanis Obomsawin, National Film Board

Tools of Struggle for Domination by Domestic Insurgents

National domination is assumed by the state. Where the state's domination is contested it is either by domestic or foreign groups. I will focus my discussion here on domination in its relation to domestic groups.

The state is the only legitimate source of violence. This violence serves to punish, threaten and serve as a warning to others. Where domestic groups resort to violence there shall be said to be three types: Guerrilla, Terrorist and Gangster/Bandit.

The guerilla and terrorist group both spring from a political ideology or way of defending a social group. This behavior is politics on another level. They are distinguished from one another by their treatment of the masses. The guerilla tends to minimize civilian casualties and leans toward disruption of the state's mechanisms and military targets.

The terrorist, in short, may have the same goals as the guerilla, but believes the masses to be guilty of passive acquiescence and complicity with the state and so, they too, become targets of terror.

The gangster/racketeer/bandit is of the self-serving ideal-type who may use violence to increase personal or family financial gain. As significant as this interest is, I will deal with the other two.

In the end, the failure or success of the insurgents lies in their ability to win and sustain mass popular support. This becomes a struggle for the domination of the human mind. The most effective propaganda wins. There are two kinds of propaganda: Agitative and Armed. The demagogue, dictator, freedom fighter can tend to dominate on either or both fronts. The domination of either is decisive.

Amongst the classic Marighella texts of urban guerrilla warfare, there is one type of discipline enforced by execution when it comes to spies and officials of the opposition but there is little, outside the role of liberation propaganda, in insurgency manuals to address a significant possible problem so outlined by Gann: **"Many advocates of urban guerrilla warfare put special trust in an armed alliance between marginal intellectuals and marginal men of the slums. They overlook, however, the extreme difficulties of enforcing discipline among two groups which, by their very nature, resist discipline in its various forms."** [26]

Counter-insurgency analysts seem to agree that whether guerrilla or terrorist groups are liberation movements, anti-imperialist in non-democratic countries, or anti-imperialistic in democratic industrial counties, that failure to win common support or overestimating mass support is a principle cause of failure where insurgent groups fail and their frequency of this is high.

Had Max Weber the opportunity to converse with Marshall McLuhan, they might have found the makings of a good theory that fits between what Weber thought was the fall of the German University system and the system of communications that McLuhan was thinking about with respect to domination of contemporary North American culture.

The face and presence of the modern media communications unit (NBC, CBC, Disney, Hollywood, the Star System, the near monopolies of Southam,

---

[26] Lewis H. Gann. *Guerrillas in History*, p. 81

Thompson & Black) was arguably certainly one of "charismatic genius". The proximity of 'political leaders' to the means of producing and distributing the 'message' has been well demonstrated by the eager acquiescence of the press to accept censorship during the war with Iraq in 1991.

Weber says that a "sense of civil self-esteem" and "sense of responsibility for their own actions" has an impact on 'inclination' to maintain their independence, that is resistance from some message.

resistance to any belief, stemming from a message, might be among several ideal types: Agitation-propaganda (message), armed-propaganda; No agitation-propaganda but armed-propaganda ('bomb now, rule later'); No resistance on any level; Agitation-propaganda, no armed-propaganda.

The timing of these occurrences is obviously important to the outcome of the event and each entity involved will have all the same options and this then becomes the principal arena where domination is contested or not. I think I would tend to put negotiations involving 'threats' of violence and violence in the same category.

Everybody uses the same tools to a greater or lesser extent. Assessing the situation correctly tips the balance one way or the other. Domination does, in this sense, lie in knowledge.

Gerard Chaliand, Malcolm X and Max Weber, I think, would agree that guerrilla warfare and terrorism are legitimate on this basis:

"Unless one condemns all forms of violence...Terrorism is always justified as a last resort. When up against the South African state, for example, what possible course of action is there other than a combination of political struggle (demonstrations, boycotts, sabotage, violence, etc.) and terrorism? Moreover South Africa itself is hardly in apposition to condemn the terrorism of the ANC when its own police systematically torture all suspects." [27]

---

[27] Gerard Chaliand, *Terrorism: From Popular Struggle to Media Spectacle* (London: Atlantic Highlands, N.J. Saqi Boos, 1987), p. 122

Lack of Resistance to Domination

"Malcolm X is purely the embodiment of this intuition, on the verge of despair, that all is useless; revolt is first of all the acknowledgement of an impossible situation." [28] This too, I suggest, is domination in suspension.

No matter how one reads it, one element required for successful domination is a weaker resistance. Pacifism can be as a significant a form of resistance as any other but to offer 'no ideas' can be a powerfully strong nihilistic vacuum that will absorb the most absurd belief for want of none. Let someone else do your thinking for you, perhaps. I would argue that there is no stasis, no ethical neutrality possible in the face of domination - one goes along or one doesn't because there is always social action involved.

Erika Mann's book outlines some of the methods of domination of Nazi ideals, through the use of racism, physically exhausting activity, surveillance, routine education, ignorance, and punishment for opponents. No blame is attached to those who were crushed under this

---

[28] Albert Memmi. *Dominated Men: Notes Towards a Portrait* (Boston, Beacon Press, 1968), p. 15

great wall but surely the myth of 'ethical neutrality' was not the safest pedestal for the early 1930's German education system to be taking refuge behind. Now, in this epoch concerning man's knowledge and awareness, in spite of Hegel's influence (re. Duty, Morality, Value), the belief in objectivity and freedom from ethics is an arrogant one, assuming a knowledge of right in a world filled with so much wrong.

Snack Two (for the brave and bold)

The inclusion of an irrational definition of domination is of interest because of its proximity and similarity to the rational. Starhawk, a feminist and white witch who defends the legitimacy of spells and magic, is well-placed to offer an irrational explanation. Stanley Milgram, Michel Foucault, Sigmund Freud, Max Weber and Bill Moyers all occupy positons in the foundation of her argument and awareness, plus her reliance on magicification, I believe, allow her work to be noted here.

"Power-over works like sorcery: it casts a spell on us. It changes our consciousness, clouds our vision so that we don't notice it in operation. It is the magician who distracts us with a rabbit as he saws the woman in half." [29]

Often the tools of domination are used to lend, promote and upgrade the dominant behavior. The dominating behavior can be composed of the most unspeakable

---

[29] Starhawk. *Truth or Dare*, p. 95

cruelties of Artaud or yet be masquerading behind a cartoon character, a popular song or a magic castle. That is the magic that Starhawk writes of, the smoke and mirrors of the demagogue. In some cases, it is a magnificently engineered network of belief systems that exists as a credit to the power of knowledge as ascribed by the early positivists St. Simon and Comte, who like Einstein, knew not the frequency and scale to which ideas would be put to pathological abuse.

"In the culture of domination, we are possessed without knowing it and without knowing techniques to free ourselves." [30] This is the possession that fell upon Mann's Germany (perhaps, the 'Iron Cage'), so complete that it took outside agencies to free the population from the spell and even then it is debatable as to how complete that spell-removal was.

The contention of one political group called Consolidated (a group of contemporary artists) is that America is a source of extreme domination. Their term for this brand of domination is called 'Friendly Fascism'. It is composed of large government and business concerns using methods of high technology and popular culture to enforce domination.

Elsewhere I have mentioned that one of the elements necessary for domination to work is a lack of resistance.

---

[30] Ibid., p. 96

Again, the contention of an emerging school of recent theorists who often back themselves with work derived from Noam Chomsky is that one aspect of resistance, i.e popular music, has been co-opted, purchased outright by the positivists.

.

"They have the best looks; politicians, celebrities and control mechanisms that money can buy...Our tastes have become so standardized and regulated that we no longer make any choices for ourselves, the Culture Industry does all this for us. We've become a nation of blindly accepting consumers latching on to meaningless terms like alternative, progressive, rap, house, techno. We're promised liberation but all we get is distraction." [31]

The basic gist of the argument is that major economic, political and social concerns are hell-bent on destruction, using every method of education, propaganda and force (where non-violence has been judged insufficient) to alienate, consume and maintain domination.

I suggest that domination has a greater chance of ruling if the amount of human alienation is high. Western man's alienation may be measured by drug use, domestic violence, psychosis, psychologically unhealthy scientists, pathological crime, etc. There are many indicators of human alienation and it strikes me that domination increases proportionally to the level of human alienation.

Eventually modern or post-modern culture can take precedence over traditional culture. I argue that this has already happened in North America among the dominant culture of whites and, to a lesser extent, the peoples of the First Nation.

---

[31] Consolidated a late 1980's early 1990's band, circulated pamphlet.

Television, McDonald's, Disneyland and the Academy Awards have supplanted traditional culture. The proof of this lies in the North American Water and Power Alliance meeting with the Cree from James Bay. I think it is safe to say that the Cree in Northern Quebec live closer to tradition because of their closer personal reliance on hunting, fishing and a spirituality based on living in the here-and-now, rather than fleeing existence as the 'other worldly' religions do. Until the 1970's there was a low incidence of radio, TV and telephone, not to mention modern man, in the area. How the cell phone and internet may impact James Bay culture remains to be seen.

When Hydro and Power developers offered to make great change in indigenous lives by building James Bay II they met resistance centered around culture, "**...classes do not act in history until they are armed by culture, as culture normally finds expression in setting the terms of class conflict. Resistance to oppression, like oppression itself, is invariably the union of class interest with cultural justification.**" [32]

Part of the difficulty here is Western Humanity's own alienation from traditional culture, that is, roots or, arguably, state of nature. Modern bankers, like their forebears, don't appreciate what the Cree are talking about. The alienist might think, "All the hocus-pocus about mother-earth spirit, reindeer and sweet grass

---

[32] Frederique Apffel Marglin & Stephen A. Marglin. *Dominating Knowledge* (Oxford, Clarendon Press; New York, Oxford University Press, 1990), p. 225

burning. These primitives still go to sweat lodges when modern man would seek advice and brotherhood from a dark bar and strangers that only care so long as the stimulants and depressants are flowing."

When the Cree rejected domination of technology in James Bay with Hydro projects, they were then subjected to *'industrial discipline'* [33] through the courts, media, and by way of internal factionalization.

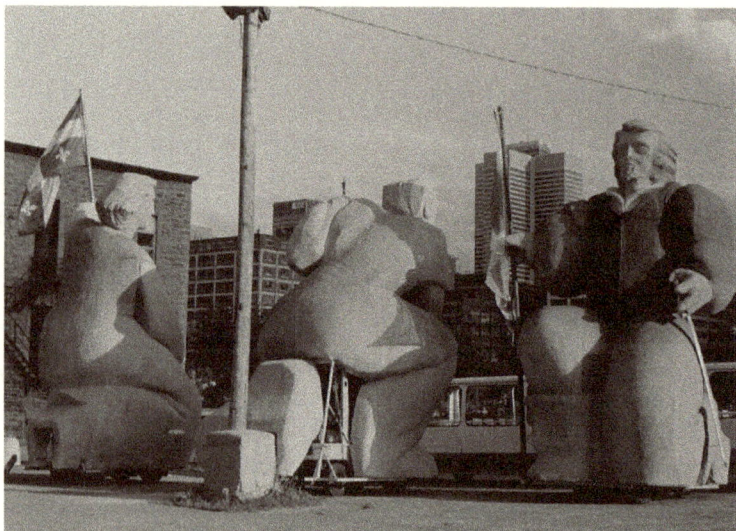

Foucault describes a modern prison: **"Each individual, in his place, is securely confined to a cell from which he is seen from in front by a supervisor; but the side walls prevent him from coming into contact with his companions. He is seen, but he does not see; he is the object of information, never a subject in communication. The most effective surveillance is unverifiable: The inmate must**

[33] Ibid., p. 54

never know whether he is being looked at any one moment; but he must be sure that he may always be so." [34]

Surveillance, then, is also a tool of domination (note the wording of the Privacy Act in the constitutional proposals) and can include self-surveillance; for example, when one compares one's life to the lives on television dramas, sitcoms, or commercials. Commercials may be set to persuade you of your dandruff and odors. Are people talking about your complexion? Are you as successful as the Hipster who takes his father out for a $50.00 lunch? How does that make you feel? When we compare our wants, needs, desires and physical forms to those of the people within commercial advertisements, we are engaged in a form of self-surveillance. And the sanctions, frankly, threaten to damn us to hell. Do the shows, programs or movies we watch differ that much from a commercial? Does the knowledge of surveillance impact the behavior of shoplifters or deter crime?

How close we come to conforming and how much we desire to conform to abstract and seemingly invisible rules that can't be, as yet, rated and measured on an empirical level is magic. **"The nasty magic of domination is done with mirrors. What is not mirrored in us, what is not seen, tends to disappear."** [35]

---

[34] Starhawk. *Truth or Dare*, p. 119
[35] Ibid., p. 120

Banuri hints at this growing interest in the irrational in his paper on *Development and The Politics of Knowledge: A critical Interpretation of the Social Role of Modernization Theories in the Development of the Third World*. He outlines several reasons for the loss of faith in or failure to believe in the 'West is Best' among underdeveloped nations. One of these is as follows: **"Escalation of the irrational arms race between the two superpowers and the accompanying intensification of belligerent rhetoric, despite widespread popular resistance have created doubts about the ability of the rational model [western] even to ensure the survival of the species."** [36] If this way of thinking became commonplace it would allow magic to come back into the world.

"Often, however, paradigms maintenance is ensured by the 'policing' efforts of the orthodoxy, through which innovation can ultimately be incorporated into older paradigms." [37]

If the jury system is in itself a form of magic because of the idea that agreement amongst 12 peers determines reality then jury nullification is a magic tool to oppose the 'policing efforts of the orthodoxy.'

Domination by Secret Demagoguery

Under tools of dominance or domination Weber points out some of the tools of demagoguery: telegrams,

---

[36] Marglin & Marglin. *Dominating Knowledge*, p. 31

[37] Ibid., p. 35

speeches, and, what I'm sure he would have approved of a meaning 'social communication', i.e. television, videos, blogs, records, tapes, texting, discs, and whatever else might carry the message of the demagogue. Could that demagogue be an institution? It is less clear and certainly less examined as to the proximity of the demagogue to the intended and unintended target audience. Where the secret police exist, there is potential for mysterious doings. (see p. 8)

A pipeline of communication is necessary for the demagogues' ideas to come to dominance and that can be separate from the demagogue as a human being. Yet if this were possible, someone or some human creation could exercise domination over some person, group, or society, complete with sanctions for disobeying (where they are built into the demagogue's belief system) and be a demagogue and operate in secret; altogether a significant situation. We might consider placing a remote cyber-hacker threat in this category. The mysterious origins of urban legends are testament to the secret origins of the initiator of tales, rumors and ideas. This is generally not domination, however, as there are no sanctions for disbelieving. The advantage to the secret demagogue is in not being held accountable for actions.

"Many believed that the country was drifting into a state in which its most pressing social problems could be solved only by extreme measures of either the political right or left. The

universities were unable to remain islands on which the unpolitical scholar and scientist could live in seclusion from the fierce agitation mounting on all sides. Not only were students disturbed by the uncertainty of future employment and inevitably concerned with political issues...students began to ferment unrest and provoke violence inside the universities." [38]

Lilge is referring to Hitler and the past, Nazi students (the extremely politically incorrect) and Germany in the mid 1930's, and Lilge felt that the university system, by means of its annual conference in 1932 and 1933, could have expressed a 'non-confidence in National Socialism' that could have increased the intellectual resistance against what was to follow. Although Lilge doesn't make specific reference to what the clue might have been that things were soon going to take a nose-dive for German education we have one that corresponds with that year from Erika Mann's book. There was one Dr. Bernhard Rus who had belonged to the Nazi Party since 1922. In February 1933 he was appointed the Prussian Minister of Culture. In the winter of 1933 he declared *"...all teachers of non-Aryan or Jewish descent were relieved of their posts."* [39] In February 1934 he was appointed the Director of Education, and in April of that same year Rus was made the Reich Minister of Science, Education and Culture.

---

[38] Frederic Lilge. *The Abuse of Learning: The Failure of the German University* (New York, Macmillan Co., 1948), p. 163
[39] Erika Mann. *School for Barbarians*, p. 45

Conclusion

Like Weber and Mann, Lilge in his epilogue points out the folly of political neutrality in the face of rhetoric and propaganda that forces the true scholar to sit up and gag.

If I may be allowed to make a stretch, I include this statement: **"In a dictator's world, even scientific inquiry, having rendered its destructive service must eventually become suspect as the last source of critical thought and nonconformity."** [40]

A peculiar role for the university, in terms of analyzing and practising domination, begins to emerge when we examine domination with the tools provided by Weber, Kant, Hegel, Mann and others and, where applicable, their thoughts on the purpose and use of the University system. The university at its best is a flower of knowledge no less important than any other in the search for truth and resistance towards wrongdoing. That being said: There arises, periodically, in the human story, pivotal moments in time and history where the silence of imposing on public affairs may be justly broken but it is not likely to be founded on the empirical evidence of future hindsight, which doesn't exist but only on the heart, the irrational spirit/magic from within that declares a statement and a hand signal.

---

[40] Op. cit., p. 166

Rousseau and Canada

In my examination *of The Social Contract* by J.J. Rousseau I thought it would be fruitful to contrast some of Rousseau's ideas about the individual and society against the same theme but within the context of a package provided by the Canadian Government known as *'Economic and Constitutional Proposals, Shaping Canada's Future.'*

I will first do this by identifying and defining five points. Then I will illustrate a dimension of each point for clarity. Finally, I will compare it with a similar point in the *Canadian Proposal*.

The purpose of this comparison is to probe specific aspects of Rousseau's thought and not to condense *the Constitutional Proposals* to a few brief pages.

Aspects of a Social Contract

Definitions of the state, freedom, property, law, and what constitutes consensus are vital to the formation of any society. Even if the law is unreasonable, the people divided into slave camps, all property belonging to the King, and the state one of heavy handed coercion, as long as all these elements are known beforehand and part of public knowledge there will be more order than chaos.

Rousseau is acutely aware that man may create any society he chooses, even one that doesn't suit him. In *The Social Contract* Rousseau tries to provide a set of guidelines that would go to support a society governed by that which is for the greater good and bound with strong moral duty.

The Social Pact

This I take to be the oral, visual, or written thing that defines the responsibility between the individual and the civil state. The social pact or contract serves to both explain and solve a problem relating to the coming together of people.

"To devise a form of association which will defend and protect the person and possessions of each associate with all the collective strength, and in which each is united with all, yet obeys only himself and remains as free as before." [41]

This statement of course is indeed the Holy Grail of constitutional reform and we are provided with a brief blue print to attain it by incorporating the following ideas.

The social actor surrenders his person and all his things to the social community, nothing is held in reserve, all is

---

[41] *The Essential Rousseau*, trans. Lowell Bair, Meridian, 1983, p. 17

surrendered. If this ideal state should be threatened, the citizen has a moral, dutiful, and legal obligation to protect the state and follow orders to do so. If he does not, he forfeits citizenship or suffers some penalty.

If I understand, society, in return, gives itself to each man and will defend the individual's right to keep what he has and have what he needs. Rousseau considers neither the individual nor society to be an abstract thing. I think he does imply however, that both the individual and society must be flexible and tolerant. No one scholar appears to have an absolute definition of this.

Where the individual's rights begin and end and society's right to intervene with individual desires, I believe, lies the notion of tolerance. There is no easy or apparent formula here. Perhaps in this social state of Rousseau's if all things were equal, if the want was less, tolerance would go up. On the other hand, his state smacks of uniformity and perhaps any deviance would stand out that much more.

Perhaps everyone could do whatever they want with their lives and it would be up to society to be flexible and tolerant enough to provide space, sustenance, and some commitment to guarantee that individuals have their requirement met in exchange for belonging to society. This is the social contract which among others would be subject to and confined by the state, freedom, property, law and the first agreement.

In *The City and Man*, Leo Strauss interprets Rousseau by saying, "**...the social contract which creates society is the basis of morality,**" and that, "**...the core of morality is the good will as distinguished from the fulfillment of all duties**" and that "**...morality means autonomy.**" [42]   Moral duty he feels, for Rousseau, is the establishment of egalitarianism.

The Social Contract or Pact has everything to do with how man participates in society. It is the establishment of a moral code. There is both a general and a particular will, that, being the difference between a social and an individual will. The problem is identifying between a social and an individual will and also identifying a legitimate general will. Rousseau would say that the general will is always legitimate.

In Canada, within our Proposal, we almost duplicate Rousseau's idea and like him are just as vague.

"**One person's right may occasionally have to be limited when it conflicts with the rights and interest of others or of the community as a whole.**" [43]

---

[42] *The City and Man*, Leo Strauss, Chicago, Rand McNally & Company, 1964, p.40

[43] *Shaping Canada's Future Together*, Minister of Supply and Services Canada, 1991, p. 3

Berger – Thrills and Chills

It seems like a valid concept. All Rousseau or the Canadian Charter is doing is to provide an intent, a direction of thought to consider when applying the law. Again, I take Rousseau's point that the law is an expression of morality. We will do things up to the point that others take an interest or are affected. I could go on and on but I would end up dancing on the head of a pin and in the end I would have to offer up 145 or so years of Canadian legal code. Under our laws we strive to legislate and define what constitutes freedom and infringement. Over time we have developed a body of law and it is this body of law which has defined where individual rights infringe on the greater community. This I believe is the body of law that Rousseau feels would give the Citizens moral freedom were they to be part of its formation.

The Civil State

"The passage from the state of nature to the civil state produces a remarkable change in man by substituting justice for instinct in his conduct and giving his acts the morality they previously lacked." [44]

In Rousseau's Civil State he doesn't allow man to grab anything he wants through force out of impulse. This is the state of nature he left behind in option for greater overall comfort and security. Here Rousseau discusses the difference between natural freedom and civil freedom.

[44] *The Essential Rousseau*, p. 20

Natural freedom again smacks of the state of nature where man is free of many moral and sentimental bonds. With civil freedom one has control over things and oneself. The idea or result of civic freedom is a stability that is less wild and more predictable to others. If we are to form a social contract and a civil state, we accept that the state of nature is left behind.

There are controls regarding civil freedom and ownership of possessions. For the state to have legitimacy it must always prove the vitalness for appropriation of property. One works to create something or exchange something in the market and that thing is fairly owned by him. Should another grab it and run unjustly then the state should applaud the effort to return the object and should itself make some effort to return it to the rightful owner. When Rousseau makes reference to possession and ownership I believe he does so within the context that Locke did, basically for a thing to be yours you must have received it through gift or labour. Something moral has occurred to allow one to have and keep this thing.

Moral freedom is defined by obedience to self-imposed law vs *'impulsion by appetite'*. [45] In *The Civil State*, Rousseau feels man will have a greater sense of moral freedom if he is obeying laws that define his behavior and he was instrumental in creating those laws. It stands to reason

---

[45] Ibid, p. 21

that if we're not all going to spend all our time nit picking at every interpretation of precedent and fact that this ideal state will need a short list of laws that are understandable to the average farmhand and the average state bureaucrat or we will have a minimum of citizen involvement.

When he talks of 'substituting justice for instinct' he makes clear that they are separate and come out of a social order. Rousseau has this sense of justice that comes about out of a keen sense of mature deliberation and the least amount of individual vested interest. Justice shall be meted out for the good of all and not by the wronged husband against the adulterous wife. The craftsman who has his property taken will not be the judge of how to deal with the thief. This is the justice that comes out of determining the most good.

The Civil State, however, is as much a state of mind as it is any particular document. Rousseau warns us in not trying to create an instrument good for all time. For as time goes on the general will of the people is bound to change through circumstance, maturity, and the unexpected. Rousseau's civil state tries to avoid the knee jerk reaction to a situation and leans towards reason.

We have a sense of justice in Canada in that our law determines that someone is innocent until proven guilty and that the person or jury who determines culpability is sufficiently removed from the situation to make a judgement not based on passion. However, I believe that the average individual in this country has been extremely removed from the creation of the law itself. I don't accept that the occasional plebiscite or radio phone in or letter campaign is sufficient for guiding legal policy in a fair or sophisticated manner. Further more, within the body of Constitutional Proposals there is no mechanism other than representational democracy to resolve questions of what is acceptable or unacceptable to the body politic. You will notice that this very system of parliamentary democracy is also proposed to be entrenched with the Charter of Rights. I believe this is a blind spot.

Rousseau may not have been able to conceive of a society where every member has a potential to be involved in the making of law due to technological innovations but if our constitution is going to survive long into the future it will make allowance for this. According to Rousseau we have not yet achieved the best civil state.

Real Property

"Every man has a natural right to everything necessary to him, but the juridical title that makes him the owner of one piece of property excludes him from all others. Having received his share, he must limit himself to it and can name no further claim to what is held in common." [46]

---

[46] *The Essential Rousseau*, p. 21

If we are going to limit people to their fair share, then I suppose we also must limit people to a share to start with. Rousseau was no so overt as to generally distribute the King's lands but he was so clear that no one should have to overcome a barrier to ownership due to someone else's excess. It strikes me that to take this an extra step it would be pretty easy for the average blue collar worker to say that bank interest prevents him from owning his own home. It might not be reasonable to pay for a house three times over 25 years. It might prohibit one from ownership.

The Canadian Charter agrees with Rousseau that the state comes first in regards to property, we see here that, **"The federal spending power is not defined in the Constitution but it has been confirmed very clearly by the Supreme Court. It is inferred from the federal government's comprehensive taxing power and its control over the public 'debt and property."** [47]

And there we lose him...

Allowing the individual to be the repository of public wealth is part of the argument that would give the factory worker control over the means of production and a real stake in the company. In fact, this worker would have greater control over the products and how they're made than the fellow that opts out and doesn't contribute in any way to society. The state still has the power to

---

[47] *Shaping Canada's Future Together*, p. 40

appropriate the factory to make what instruments are necessary as the result of some condition important to the country. In between times the nation doesn't lose because the factory is controlled by 1000 people as opposed to a few majority share-holders. The factory is still there regardless of who owns it.

Debt, with Rousseau's concept of property might become more a matter for the Social Police than for a Banker. If we have equality and freedom for what reason would someone have to go in debt? With what tools may someone collect a debt? I can see how the determination of who gets property, how much and when, really underpins so much of Rousseau. It is after all the very place in which we all live. We rent our property, or own our property, have no property, or owe money for our property. Rousseau again reaffirms that the state is the ultimate controller of the property. We should have our property by determining the need to have it and what you have done to it in terms of enhancing, maintaining, or somehow working it to remain autonomous. This is to separate your property from the public park and its right of way passage, from the apartment you rented maintained, painted, and fixed up for the past 10 years or the tree house your kids built on public lands and now want to move into by right of labour and possession.

Rousseau would limit the share of land that people receive. This is, for our Canadian society, radical egalitarianism. Limitations on ownership are generally met with loud cries from the powerful and propertied. I suppose this would put a cap on inheritance, labour, and gift as it applies to accumulation of property. In time, perhaps people would devote themselves to something other than accumulation as a means of determining whether existence is meaningful.

He didn't argue away inequality. Regardless of what system attains its potential it will not immediately eradicate the inequality that was there immediately prior to the change. I think his vision, were it to be implemented, would freeze, for an instant, the present process and cease any backward motion. In time with greater stability the system would allow a majority to have relative comfort.

This brings us to law which determines property.

Various Systems of Law

"If we seek to determine precisely what constitutes the greatest good of all, which should be the goal of every system of law, we find that it can be reduced to these two main elements: freedom and equality." [48]

---

[48] *The Essential Rousseau*, p. 45

Freedom and equality are very popular. Whose freedom and whose equality turn out to be the big contest. Many wars and atrocities have been committed to in the name of freedom and equality. I think though it would be fair to say that these disputable and elusive qualities are often determined by certain vested interests that are not in keeping with the general will.

What we will and will not protect, entrench, and idealize will forever be determined by Abraham Lincoln's statement, *"You can fool all of the people some of the time and some of the people all of the time but you can't fool all of the people all of the time."* Rousseau allows that the people can be led down the garden path and be fooled but he sees it as a temporary point in time and that regardless of the law, the general will is a spirit of its own and it is either served or not served by the spirit of the law.

So long as things are not ideal and social engineering doesn't go in the direction of some nightmarish vision of perverted moral purpose, aka Brave New World or domination by artificial machine intelligence, then the propagandists and the rabble will always work themselves up into a frenzy and push for change.

What concept people are to believe is not something that can be carved in stone for all time. Perhaps if it was a very short list that reflected certain unarguable definite aspects of the human condition but even here we are playing God and whenever we try to legislate the future we always work with a blind spot of that which we can not know.

"As for equality, the word must not be taken to imply that power and wealth are to be exactly the same for everyone, but rather that power shall not reach the point of violence and shall never be exercised except by virtue of rank and law, and that, so far as wealth is concerned, no citizen shall be rich enough to be able to buy another, and none poor enough to be forced to sell himself. This presupposes moderation with regard to property and influence on the part of those in high position, and moderation with regard to avarice and covetousness on the part of those in humbler circumstances." [49]

Without limits, property could determine law and Rousseau, by talking of limits, thought to reduce the impact of the accumulated property of the individual in creating conditions contrary to the general will.

This is the ideal state. If one hears a family dispute next door or the local store is being robbed, one simply dials 911 and the social engineering police show up, assess the situation, provide the lawbreaker with an appropriate job, income, prescriptions or therapy. Does the householder require a shot of a tranquilizer or the like or should he choose a job with less stress? Perhaps the whole family should be put into therapy. This is a non-violent scenario.

---

[49] Ibid. p. 45

Coercion could be limited to the briefest restraint and a solution. We hope the general will would not allow for the sociological and psychological profession to be used as an instrument of repression, as it was in the old Soviet Union, to hound intellectuals and dissidents. At any rate contemporary prisons could provide a more useful function as empty museums of the past.

This doesn't solve what to do with the pathological killer or other extremely abhorrent individuals but it does separate that which can be helped from that which presently can't. Again, all things being equal, motivation and opportunity for deviance would naturally be lessened.

The postal clerk will not represent himself as ambassador nor will he dole out punishment to a convicted criminal. The ballet instructor will not pose as the Queen. Power will be limited to those who need it on the level required to fulfill their responsibility.

With Rousseau we will have a leader. In his ideal state we will have elected him or her through some manifestation of the general will or there will eventually be social disorder. It stands to reason that vested interest will be of less account if all are limited in their accumulation of property.

In my mind then, the state will provide what is required for an individual to lead a pleasant and fine life. If private interests do not offer sufficient inducement for the individual to give up his time and participate in labour on someone else's behalf, then that is the private interest's loss.

The naïve and reactionary have a nightmare vision of 30 million Canadians sitting in front of 30 million video screens drinking 30 million cans of beer and cashing 30 million welfare cheques for life. Regardless of drugs, entertainment and other diversions (which are often an expression of alienation) the human being does not have a history of collectively doing 'nothing no how for nobody'. Humans like to do things and Rousseau tries to reveal a manner that allows for their greatest potentiality.

I think it possible to unfold part of Rousseau's concept like this. Once land or property is legitimately gained, the way it may be preserved for the family and thereby contribute to social cohesion and community is if that house, plot, condo, principle living residence can not be risked through collateral, mortgage, debt, or exchange except to exchange it for some other form or type of principle living residence.

Property is a thing either owned by the individual or the state and none except the state may expropriate it and then for the good of all. He who has lost property does so only temporarily and the state intends to return the same land with compensation or strike some fair deal where the individual regains autonomy.

The law is flexible and empathetic with the land and its contents. It stands to reason that any set of laws given to the body politic must reflect certain peculiarities of the land and people. Social laws in relation to water use in the desert will be different from those in a society surrounded by a fresh water lake. It would be reasonable to allow a cattle farmer more land where the soil is sparse, for nourishing his her, and less land where the soil is rich and fertile. If each man has a hundred heard, the farmer with the richest soil has less claim to land the same size as the farmer who has the more adverse conditions.

The override clause of our Charter known as the 'not withstanding clause' is a superb example of law being set by those other than the people. The power to revoke the applicability of the social contract, in Canada, resides not in the individual, family, or community but among the majority members of Parliament or the Provincial legislature. This system of decision making is itself also entrenched in the *Proposals*.

We Must Always Go Back To A First Agreement

"There will always be a great difference between subduing a multitude and governing a society. If separate individuals are successively subjugated to the domination of one man, whatever their number may be, I see only a master and his slaves, not a people and its ruler." [50]

If we are going to agree that we are working towards a civil state under law, then the body politic must have more freedom than a slave. The body politic also calls itself something. It has some kind of identity usually based on some form of communication. We have often defined ourselves by language. He is Italian. She is French. Perhaps in the future he will become DOS, she will become BASIC and that guy will become Binary. Languages change. In the Soviet Union we witness geographical boundaries of new nations being decided largely by language, religion, and geography.

In Canada, I will say that our first agreement must go back to the British North America Act and then the Canadian Charter of Rights. Prior to either of those documents our initial ancestral agreements as Canadians will be revolved around common languages and business interests; ie the Hudson Bay Company, various Railway companies.

"The Charter ensures that laws restrict freedom as little as it reasonably possible. Freedom and fulfillment of the individual are limited only by the need for all individuals to have the same freedom and all that goes with it.

---

[50] *The Essential Rousseau*, p. 15

"The purpose of equality rights, the Canadian Supreme Court has said, is to remedy or prevent discrimination against Groups suffering social, political or legal disadvantage.

"In the Canadian experience it has not been enough to protect only universal individual rights. Here, the Constitution and ordinary laws also protect other rights accorded to individuals as members of certain communities…The fact that community rights exist alongside individual rights in our Constitution goes to the very heart of what Canada is all about." [51]

Our agreement strives for equality, freedom, and the determination of tolerance. Canadians come together under this contract and agree to serve the needs of others under it.

In response to meeting 'certain Canadian objectives' the Government of Canada proposes the establishment of a Council of the Federation. This is composed of federal, provincial and territorial governments. This council's collaboration is to decide use of federal money. Significantly this council of phantoms would have no permanent staff or headquarters nor be elected to the position by the body politic.

Since the council is specifically not directly elected to the posts by the electorate, and since its mandate is the control and direction of federal money, this represents

---

[51] *Shaping Canada's Future*, p. 3-4

and example of Rousseau's 'degeneracy of the Government.'

"It is not the government that contracts, but the state; I mean that the state as a whole dissolves and another is formed inside it, composed only of the members of the government." [52]

When Rousseau talks about the government contracting he meant 'from the larger to the smaller' and specifically felt that power descended more into the hands of an aristocracy from the wider arena of democracy. He felt that this contracting was a signal.

Now the new proposed limits on the senate in regards to what falls within their mandate, and the new powers given to the Council of the Federation, and the manner in which these people are chosen, I believe are indications of this degeneracy.

All things come about through a general will even if it is the general will being suppressed. Rousseau's ideal state could come about as easily as any other, dependent on the kind(s) of social engineering taking place in society. Fundamentally people have to want, they have to need a particular thing before they can ever have it.

A society's morality, law, civil code, property, and social contract are each determined as much by the other as any single concept. They all touch each other on some level

---

[52] *The Essential Rousseau*, p. 72

and so increase in their profundity and importance. Rousseau's ideas have much to inspire the disenfranchised should they have/create both the opportunity and eagerness to listen. His views down through the centuries have entered our most basic agreements as a society and provide a challenge to be met for the future civil and moral freedom of the citizen.

Could Emile Durkheim and Max Weber Have Developed Sufficient Charisma to Get on the Other Side of a Burning Police Car and Squeeze Off Hot Lead to Protect Timothy Leary from the Cops?

I am interested in the charisma of individuals and the events that lead up to their acceptance. I am interested in barriers that obstruct their path. It is especially interesting to deal with the subject in light of the current world climate. To this end I have broken down the study of charisma into seven categories: Domination and Education; Domination and Rational Economics; Deindividuation As A Threat; Media; The Environment; Style; and Deviance.

I will limit the discussion of charisma to that part of it which draws on value rational orientation. This is defined by Max Weber as, "...the actions of persons who, regardless of possible cost to themselves, act to put into practice their convictions of what seems to them to be required by duty,

---

[53] *Economy and Society*, p. 25

honour, the pursuit of beauty, a religious call, personal loyalty, or
the importance of some 'cause' no matter in what it consists." [53]

The study of charisma necessarily involves the study of
deviance, consensual validation, interpersonal behavior,
group dynamics, and a plethora of other disciplines
interpreting socio-psychocultural phenomenon.

I feel, however, that the greatest immediate benefit of
the study of charisma will be derived by centering
discussion on the works of Max Weber, Emile Durkheim,
Edward Sutherland, a general peak at group dynamics and
early work by Timothy Leary.

Charisma, wherever it is found, appears to be most
noticed in the actions and behavior of leaders. This leads
to a general questioning on when are leaders required?
Under what conditions is a person most likely to become a
leader? Is charisma spontaneous? Is charisma part of a
process or the end result? Where is it on the continuum of
human phenomenon? Who are most likely to become
charismatic? Under what conditions may charisma gain
acceptance? Can charisma be received with hostility? Is
charisma required to remove the uncomfortable feelings
within an anomic situation? Does charisma have a
tendency to appear with greater frequency in anomic
than non-anomic organization? Can a person have bags of
charisma and not be followed? If people follow a social
actor does it presuppose that the social actor is a leader

or possessing of charisma? Can one be a charismatic leader without desiring it? Can charisma be separated from leadership?

Roy Berger's Theoretical Process of Charisma

<u>Four Charismatic Problems.</u> 1) There is a state of anxiety. 2) There is a recognizable problem. 3) There is consensual validation of the problem and or some kind of symbolic interaction with it. 4) Learned behavior and social actions in accordance with Sutherland's Principles of Differential Association. [see page 82-83].

<u>Four Charismatic Answers.</u> 1) Guilty behavior turns into tertiary deviance by all social actors. 2) There is consensual validation by all social actors. 3) There is an unanimously agreed upon defined goal. 4) The leader provides a defined solution.

It is quite possible that the process of charisma, from the initial need found in anxiety to the end result, of no need which was produced by its defined solution, follows the problem/answer pattern listed above. The followers don't need to have the knowledge of how to solve the problem. I think they only need to believe that the person they have vested with leadership has the capability to do so. I will also show that both collective and individual behavior are related, that charisma is possible from most any participant depending on the proximity/degree to which that social actor is along the continuum outlined above.

There appears to be a relationship between charisma and interpreting the behavior and actions of others. It appears to be related to a need within all sets of affected social actors.

Charisma is a virtue available under most extraordinary circumstances to most people. When charisma falls to that tertiary deviant who inspects his own navel and then, according to Weber, casts away all manner of rational economic concept then that social actor may become dissident in the field of his concentration. His/her popularity and following will be equal to their ability to rely on internal controls, social graces and to have selected or been selected by a population that is ready to leave rational economics (and thus a degree of exploitation) behind.

Some threats to rational economics include unpopular war, discontent among the agrarian class and nationalist division within a nation state. But basically a threat to rational economics is anything that weakens either currency or the agencies which support the notions of capital accumulation. The nation state is cemented together with bank and treasury bonds, tax collecting and trade deals and the charisma of paper money over precious metals.

Just For Fun; A List of Social Actors Who May Have Exhibited Charismatic Traits

Poet – Allen Ginsberg, Bob Dylan

Writer – Jack Kerouac, Joseph Goebbels, Ken Kesey, Sinclair Lewis.

Artist – Jackson Pollock, Salvador Dali, Gary Trudeau, Ellen Gabriel.

Politician – John F. Kennedy, Pierre Elliot Trudeau, Louis Riel, Nelson Mandela, (abolitionist) John Brown, Che Guevara, Mother Jones, Malcolm X.

Soldier – Audie Murphy, Ronald (Lasagna) Cross, Milton Born With A Tooth, Edward Snowden, Irish Republican Army soldiers.

General – Eisenhower, Charles de Gaulle, General Westmoreland, Fidel Castro, Menachem Begin.

Educational Professor - Abimael Guzman , Timothy Leary, Angela Davis

Actor – Jane Fonda, Lenny Bruce

Journalist – Bob Woodward and Carl Bernstein, Gordon Sinclair, Hunter S. Thompson, Julian Assange.

Radio D.J. – Wolfman Jack, Murray The K.

Social Control Agent – J.Edgar Hoover, Senator Eugene McCarthy.

Worker – Lech Walesa, Tankman (June 5, 1989 Tiananmen Square, China)

Student – Abbey Hoffman, Jerry Rubin, Students for a Democratic Society.

Doctor – Henry Morgentaler, Benjamin Spock, Norman Bethune.

Musicians – Sex Pistols, Grateful Dead, The Beatles

Lawyer – Gandhi, Julias Grey the action of pro-bono billing?

Spiritual – Mother Theresa, L. Ron Hubbard, Reverend Sun Myung Moon, Martin Luther King.

Place – refugee camp, squatted land, right of way passage, historically disputed ownership of land.

Accountants – Makers of counterfeit money, large economic swindles, pyramid schemes.

Media – The internet, pornography, banned information The Pentagon Papers, WikiLeaks.

Criminals – serial killers, organized crime leaders, prison rioters.

Many of the people on the list fall into several categories. All were controversial in the context of their time. All had a wide following or still do. All made value rational judgements and had a fundamental impact on the structure of society or morality. These people had goals and communicated those goals to others in a time of economic, moral or political crises.

To be clear, I present the basis for Durkheim's theory of anomie. We must understand that an anomic situation is indeed one of crises. This can be a dangerous situation because it will likely be exploited by all types of charismatic leaders.

Durkheim's Anomie Theory

Anomie

"The individual has little or no guidelines of what is expected. Anomie is a situation in society where the norms of society are unclear and no longer applicable to the times in which we live. It is a time of double messages and no clear leadership." [54]

Source > Independent Variable > Dependent Variable

Social Change > Anomie > Anomic Suicide

(normative breakdown)

Rapid abrupt social change, ie: industrial revolution leads to a lack of norms in terms of urbanization has an impact on suicide rates.

Forty years later Thomas Merton revises Durkheim's Anomie theory.

---

[54] Professor Horiwich, Social Deviance Lecture, Concordia University, October, 1990

Goals Means Disjunction leads to Anomie which can have a reciprocal agreement with deviance as in, conformity, innovation ritualism, retreatism, or rebellion.

When writing of charisma, I choose to do so in the context of what I believe to be the dissolving of the nation state. The jeopardies facing today's world are immense and real enough to threaten the existence of humanity itself. These dangers exist as potential fuel for the charismatics, regardless of their intent, politics or eccentricity.

I do not believe that it would be out of place to suggest that the world of 1991 is heading into or presently in a state of anomie. Presently more than 100 countries are at war or in serious conflict on their own soil. Most significantly Yugoslavia, South Africa, East Germany, New Guinea, Moldavia, Armenia and Peru are in a state of extreme unrest led by indentured slaves, students, farmers, squatters and the general public. Recent events at Oka, Quebec, Washington D.C., Port Aux Basques Newfoundland, and Pemberton British Columbia in addition to the anger of 636,000 recipients of welfare cheques in the Montreal area also suggest that faith in traditional guidelines is dissolving.

Charisma

One is blessed with charisma if one attains a position of decision making without benefit of traditional means. We may observe that charismatic leaders are those who are sent to jails as often as they are sent to the grave. Hence the powerful impose the derogatory label of 'rebel' as opposed to 'leader' on the charismatic to try and limit the growth of his following. The charismatic deviant is one who acts as if their goals are legitimated because they voice the desires of an unacknowledged or un-empowered group in society. Where the nation borders of the charismatic's society are situated and where it is desired that it should be situated usually determines the probability and extent of conflict.

A charismatic poet like Ginsberg may howl from a narrow table top while a charismatic warrior like Lasagna may raise a rifle from atop an overturned police car. Both have charisma.

"With the vanishing of the genuine roots of charisma the everyday power of tradition and the belief in its sanctity regain their preponderance." [55] The key here has to do with the legacy of the charismatic and their followers, their

[55] *Economy and Society*, University of California Press, Max Weber, ed. Roth & Wittich, p. 1127

monument. The solution may lie in creating a new tradition as powerful as the framing of a constitution in order that a new magical ruler does not have to be constantly contrived to win the belief of the masses and most especially to limit or entirely curtail the human misery that often accompanies change.

Weber felt that the hindrance precluding direct participation of the masses with controlling the political destiny of an elected party was due to technical reasons. Today's technological inventions could remove this hurdle to public control of governmental policy. A type of voting card preserving the secret ballot, similar to the modern electronic chip bank card complete with an ID number could remove the need for the type of representation we have today in parliament. The great unwashed could be given direct control over the destiny of the nation. The legislation of morality, economy and society could be as fluid as the tyranny of the majority. Although it doesn't preclude the participation and influence of snake oil salesmen it is but one example that could remove the need or reinforce the need for small elite groups controlling democracy, who, Weber admits, can be subject to 'horse trading', questionable agendas, and closed door dealings. Empowering the people through technology has become a possibility where in Weber's time it was much more limited. [56]

Domination, Education and Charisma

The breakdown of discipline is in part what created a vacuum for the charismatic to fill in the first place. The blind obedience of subjects is possible over the long term only through an education program that provides a set of ideas, beliefs, and direction that will lead to a minimum of dissent. The university system has come into wide use around the world. By its very nature the university encourages a certain amount of dissent. However, by limiting enrollment to as few a number of lower class students as possible education may be reserved for an executive elite who are often taught through ancestry and educators that their role in life is to maintain the status quo and ensure a large supply of willing workers to turn the wheels of industry.

"The status and privileges of the universities were granted to them by the military-aristocratic ruling class, and were not achieved as part of the growth of free enterprise...a precarious status based on a compromise whereby rulers of the state consider the universities as means for the training of certain types of professionals." [57] This is a form of rational education, similar to rational capitalism, ensuring a minimum of

---

[56] *Economy and Society*, p., 1128
[57] *The Scientist's Role In Society*, Page 135, Ben David, Chicago, 1984

social mobility and behooving a maximum of tolerance and patience from the workers. The potential charismatic leader would do well to seize moments of disciplinary loss and empower the masses with those elements that lead to social action. The agenda is less important than the belief of being on the winning side, this is the side of lesser anxiety.

A scientific and philosophically aware population would not give the empires of today the mandate to do what they want with natural resources nor would they be inclined to provide a rich income for their exploiters. It is only by the education (ideas, beliefs, direction) we receive that people will dedicate their lives to trivial and meaningless tasks.

People can only act on what they believe to be true and their action will be tempered/influenced by the relative strength of the coercive action directed at them, be it the physical end of a police baton or the psychological brutality of watching a clever commercial. This is part of what the charismatic leader must contend with. The charismatic's action to take this knowledge into account may be based on the sober reflection of scholarly retreat or, as likely, made during those split seconds when a mob must decide if it is to flee in panic or become a mature and cohesive group.

Sadly, long term or especially dramatic coercion can lead to wide scale conflict. Revolution, rebellion and civil wars are each fueled by separate social and economic sentiments. Within each of these lie separate aids and threats to the charismatic. [58] Lack of social graces and bias of education are significant threats to the charismatic.

We see this time and again through the evolution of the university system from the Berkeley free speech movement to *The Sir George William's Affair* or Burlington University in Vermont in 1991. In these places an educated populace battled for freedom from perceived oppression.

Deindividuation as A Threat to Charisma

"Discipline and its sister, bureaucracy, presuppose an allegiance to one other than the self, ie, an institution, state, bosses. It assumes domination by virtue of a subtle or obvious deindividuation. To observe bureaucracy is to believe in something else other than family, community, or friendship as that to appease, obey and conform to." [59]

Harry S. Sullivan, K. Horney, E. Fromm and Timothy Leary were correct in their description for the motive of personality. "Anxiety (feelings of helplessness, danger, isolation, weakness or loss of self esteem) is interpersonal because it is rooted in the dreaded expectation of derogation 8 [Derogation: a lessening or impairment (of power, law, positon, etc); detraction; the state of becoming worse and rejection by others (or by one's

---

[58] *Economy and Society*, page 1120
[59] *Economy and Society*, p.,1149

self).] "...the motivating principle of behavior is more accurately seen as 'anxiety reduction' – the avoidance of the greater anxiety and the selection of the [appreciatively] lesser anxiety." [60] The charismatic here would do well to shape the direction of motives towards the lessening of anxiety.

It is the goal of rational economics to crush individuality. Charisma is what we say an individual has if they speak believable words pointing in a particular direction without offending their followers. The charismatic acts as an individual. If their words were true and the path successful, their charisma is enhanced. Nothing may stop them but death, failure or disgrace. The time tested formula has always been to jail, shame or assassinate the charismatic should one show signs of uniting the disenfranchised, the unorganized, the distressed. This is of course, the theory of domination and fear at work which is also accelerated by disinformation programs.

The opponent of the charismatic is all and anything that stands to lose by the charismatic's acceptance. Whatever would grow anxious at its acceptance. All, bar none to be sure, will use any means to attack the charismatic.

Weber wrote of the existence of discipline within armies [6] The development of the nuclear bomb truly eradicated the need for individual combat. Yet combat continues to

---

[60] *Interpersonal Diagnosis of Personality: A Functional theory and Methodology for Personality Evaluation*, Timothy Leary, Ronald Press, 1957, page 8
[61] *Economy and Society*, p. 1151

exist. Examination of the players of war however does not show much combat taking place on the soil of the nuclear club, except in the case of sporadic guerrilla campaigns. In these cases, however the enemy of the state does not stay anywhere long enough for nuclear warfare to be of any productive benefit. Nuclear warfare is productive only in a case of institution vs institution. This type of war may also be unproductive when one thinks of the shrinking ownership of companies and their subsidiaries all over the world having an increasing vested interest against supply interruption. Banking, entertainment and manufacturing sectors revolve around supply chain management spread over a variety of nation states. The lone wolf or small disenchanted cell with access to critical weapons may have less regard for these alliances.

The Media and Charisma

The increasing centralized ownership of the media puts public information at risk in that fewer people have control over the dissemination of ideas and beliefs. The media is certainly capable of reinforcing leaders and institutions. It is no coincidence that the target of government and rebel attacks alike is often the radio, television or print presses. For other than the scholastic system, which is universally inadequate for the needs of the masses, the media represent the only flow of information outside the immediate environment of the individual.

Now then, individuals have a certain amount of control with media by way of cell phones, texting and the use of the internet. As well there are over 2 billion operating shortwave radios in use with more coming on line every year. These are lower priced tools than mass market circulation traditional press and more available to 'everyman'.

In *Politics as a Vocation*, Weber wrote about the likelihood of the journalist ascending to politics or affecting it. **"In any case, for the time being, the journalist career is not among us, a normal avenue for the ascent of political leaders, whatever attraction journalism may otherwise have and whatever measure of influence, range or activity, and especially political responsibility it may yield. One has to wait and see."** [62] It would have been interesting to have Weber's views on the rise of Rene Levesque, Adrienne Clarkson or Conrad Black's affinity with journalism and the political sphere.

Weber's views here would have been confirmed had he been able to meet with David Suzuki, a professor and journalist. Since airing his show, *The Nature of Things*, on the Amazon rain forest, the charismatic leader Chico Mendes, a spokesman for the rubber tappers featured on the program has been shot and killed. In addition, Suzuki

---

[62] *From Max Weber*, p. 98

had both his home and university office burglarized (April 1991) and a bullet put through one of his windows at home. [63] This serves as a warning to all respected educators who would dare criticize and I believe a significant signal of what direction industry can move in.

Another example of an institution putting public ideas and beliefs at risk took place in Quebec, Canada. From November 1990 to May 1991 Hydro Quebec was granted a court injunction forbidding the press to report news of existing contracts between the electric power company and aluminium smelters. The smelters would have an impact on 10,000 Cree natives around James Bay and possibly impact the ecology of the planet itself. The censorship is testimony to the favouring of the Hearts and Minds policy still used as a normal means of control. To win the people's hearts and manipulate the people's minds has long been a tool of the powerful. Interestingly enough, even though the court injunction expired, no media in the province revealed the details. And where the masses create their own medium in spite of authority, such as the democratic wall in China, it takes on legendary proportions.

A sinister weapon of war between the classes is often to be found in the cracks between propaganda and truth whether it be for the purpose of turning the wheels of

---

[63] *The Montreal Gazette*, May 18, 1991

industry, cutting sugar cane, or serving the nation state as cannon fodder, "**...for this society is almost overwhelmingly dominated by very powerful forces – constellations of people and wealth – which are committed to the ideology of exploitation, and this ideology permeates the communications media to such an extent as to be practically unchallenged.**" [64]

Our contemporary media is indeed a tool of fear, propaganda and misinformation which again is customary with the tactics of domination.

When one thinks of domination today it is important to think of the role of the journalist or the media as a whole. We accept that the concentration of media ownership has been reduced to the hands of fewer individuals, organizations and groups than in previous years. Ralph Miliband felt that there was an 'engineering of consent' [65] that is common to capitalistic societies that helps foster a belief in the status quo among the masses. This was a further scrutiny based on Marx's view that 'the class which controlled the means of production controlled the means of producing beliefs and symbols in a society.' Mind control is a cost-effective means of dominating a society. During the Vietnam war (police action) it was referred to as the 'Hearts and Minds' policy. The charismatic knows this consciously or unconsciously and

---

[64] *Politics and the Restraint of Science*, LA. Cole, Rowman Pub, 1983 p. 87
[65] *Sociology A Brief but Critical Introduction*, Anthony Giddens, Harcourt Brace Johanovich, 1987, p. 41

this is reason one why they only believe what they see for themselves.

Charisma, Domination and Rational Economics

The job of rational economic leaders is to show strength and never weaken. To encourage belief in its system by any means, be it the whips and dogs of South African police or the purchasing of the media by the military-industrial complex. General Electric, a massive marketer of weapons did just this by purchasing NBC in 1986 for $6.28 billion dollars. [66] The company which has a vested interest in making war bought the news.

Charisma may reject rational economic structure. [67] This point is well observed by noting an event in May 1967 when 18 members of the YIPPIE Party interrupted trading on the floor of the New York stock exchange by throwing dollar bills from the observer's gallery to the trading floor below. The resulting scramble for cash (between $100 and $1000) among the stock traders halted the nation's business for several minutes. This won many charismatic points for the spokesmen of the Youth International Party, Jerry Rubin and Abbie Hoffman. [68]

---

[66] *Press For Conversion*, Issue 3, 1990, p. 20

[67] *Economy and Society*, p. 1113

[68] *Revolution for the Hell of It*, by Free, Dial Press, 10th print, 1970, p. 35-38

There is a remarkable similarity between Sutherland's Rules and the revolutionary behavior of the charismatic leader and the followers. Criminal behavior is behavior so ruled by society's folkways, mores and legal norms. I believe that the value rational charismatic acts in a revolutionary way, be they poet, writer, or warrior. I believe then that it is reasonable to transpose the word criminal for the word revolutionary and find Sutherland's rules are well applicable to both.

"Sutherland's Rules of Differential Association. [69]

1. **Criminal behavior is learned.**
2. **Criminal behavior is learned in interaction with other persons in a process of communication.**

---

[69] *Deviant Behavior*, Alex Thio, 3rd edition, Harper & Row, 1990, p. 35-38

3. The principal part of the learning of criminal behavior occurs within intimate personal groups.
4. When criminal behavior is learned, the learning includes; A) techniques of committing the crime. B) The specific direction of motives, drives, rationalizations and attitudes.
5. The specific direction of motives and drives learned from definitions of the legal codes as favourable or unfavourable.
6. A person becomes delinquent because of an excess of definitions favourable to violation of law over definitions unfavourable to violation of law.
7. Differential association may vary in frequency, duration, priority, and intensity.
8. The process of learning criminal behavior by association with criminal and anti-criminal patterns involves all of the mechanisms that are involved in any other learning.
9. While criminal behavior is an expression of general needs and values it is not explained by those general needs and values, since non-criminal behavior is an expression of the same needs and values."

The Environment and its Relation to Charisma

The word environment includes the air one breathes, the soil one stands on and the water and food ingested by the individual. Psychics, shrinks, and sociologists alike agree that the environment, that is the conditions surrounding the observers and participants, affects the judgements, actions, ideas of both roles. It is worth noting that the environment affecting individuals is only limited by the observable planetary conditions, individuals, groups, and organizations who will evaluate their behavior consciously or unconsciously within this context. When talking of the sociological or psychological environment of the social actor, the modern day analyst may have to give the environment of the earth as much importance as the dysfunctional family or economic conditions of the social actor.

The very air we breathe, and water we drink is filled with the cruelty of imperialism. Here I refer to the toxins that have entered the food chain on a scale that did not exist prior to the 1950's. I mention the environment because it appears to be a concern shared by reactionaries and conservative educators alike in many countries, regardless of language, ethnicity, or locality. The air doesn't smell as good as it used to and one out of three Canadians is forecasted to die of cancer, a disease often linked with synthesized products like the depleted uranium casings that are used in war munitions.

The environment is no longer seen as strictly a national problem. It tends to be regarded as one which affects all nations. This then places environmental concerns on a global scale and so the ideas, beliefs, and actions associated with these concerns may indeed be indicative of a trend or direction that will be a common ground out weighing the present concerns of nation states. Here there lies conflict. Conflict between the heads of state and masses would be polarized by the complicity between corporations and state affairs. It would follow then that this conflict would be present or emerging in increasing numbers of nation states.

If magic is part of the irrational, and environmental group protest is a reaction against the rational economic exploitation of the environment, then in a sense an environmental group is similar to Weber's magic brotherhood. [70]   Enviro-training is similar to magic training. Witness the growing alliances taking place between traditional worshippers of Mother Earth be they white middle class intellectuals or aboriginal nations.

"The extent and direction of 'rationalization' is thus measured negatively in terms of the degree to which magical elements of thought are displaced, or positively by the extent to which ideas gain in systematic coherence and naturalistic consistency." [71]

Chaos physics, magic, and perhaps un-syncopated jazz music (were it to have existed in his time), these are the aspects of life, measurement, and tools which Weber would have sought to marginalize through empirical science and fatalistic devotion to rigid systematic thought. This has always been fertile ground for tyranny, totalitarianism, and radical nationalism. This concept was well illustrated by the Montreal poet, Leonard Cohen. **"Jazz Police are looking through my folders. Jazz Police are talking to my niece. Jazz Police have got their final orders. Jazzer, drop**

---

[70] *Economy and Society*, p. 1145
[71] *From Max Weber*, p. 50

your axe, it's Jazz Police." [72] For my money it was the Jazz Police who shot at David Suzuki.

---

[72] *I'm Your Man*, Leonard Cohen, 1987

Weber assumes the inevitability of "...**the slow death of charisma with each hour of its life due to a suffocation under the weight of material interests.**"[73] The channeling of the mass's interest from materialism to spiritualism, paganism, environmentalism or any other 'ism' has long been a challenge to the church, communists, hippies, socialists, humanists, educators and others who see the preservation and continuance of the human species in terms of enlightenment and love. I believe that the book has not yet been closed on this subject. For every Kent State University student whose flowers were circumvented by rifles (May 1970, Ohio) and the students who set themselves ablaze in protest against the police beating a student to death in South Korea (May 1991). These sorts of actions have kept the consciousness of dissent and material opposition in vigor and memory.

Charismatic Style – The Duty and Mission

"**Consensual validation is the degree of approximate agreement with a significant other person or persons which permits fairly exact communication by speech or otherwise, and the drawing of generally useful inferences about the action and thought of the other.**" [74]

"**Behavior which is related overtly, consciously, ethically , or symbolically to another human being (real, collective or imagined) is interpersonal.**" [75]

---

[73] *Economy and Society*, p. 1120

[74] *Interpersonal Diagnosis of Personality: A Functional Theory and Methodology for Personality Evaluation*, Timothy Leary, Ronald Press, 1957, p. 9

"Charisma knows only inner determination and inner restraint. The holder of charisma seizes the task that is adequate for him and demands obedience and a following by virtue of his/her mission. His success determines whether he finds them. His charismatic claim breaks down if his mission is not recognized by those to whom he feels he has been sent. If they recognize him, he is their master ...so long as he knows how to maintain recognition through 'roving' himself. But he does not derive his 'right' from their will, in the manner of an election. Rather, the reverse holds: it is the duty of those to whom he addresses his mission to recognize him as their charismatically qualified leader." [76]

It is most interesting to contrast these statements. The first by Leary, the second by Weber. Weber sees the onus of recognition, in this instance, on the potential following and appears to have a more or less clear designation between follower and followee. But Leary, I think, more clearly implies that the charismatic is responsible for communicating the message in a clear understandable manner than the audience is in understanding. In other words it is not enough to have a message but the delivery itself is an important part of the process. This disparity between delivery and reception of message may be revealed as vocabulary and concept. Just as a lawyer has to be careful not to distance himself from the jury by using concepts and words too complicated to be understood by the jury I believe it is even more so for the

[75] Ibid., p. 4
[76] *From Max Weber*, p. 246

charismatic. The value rational charismatic often works under tension, pressure, and has been selected by a group operating with a hair spring trigger, so to speak. The crowd is always after the least anxiety by the fastest route believable.

If we accept the social actor's duty not as a calling but as a normal human attribute of avoiding anxiety, then we are in agreement with both Karen Horney and Timothy Leary in that the social actor seeks the most comfortable environment that is believed to be attainable. It is important here that the charismatic not be guilty of providing false hope which in the long run may lead to status frustration.

"First working principle of interpersonal dynamics. Personality is the multilevel pattern of interpersonal responses (overt, conscious, private) expressed by the individual. Interpersonal behavior is aimed at reducing anxiety. All the social, emotional interpersonal activities of an individual can be understood as attempts to avoid anxiety or to establish and maintain self-esteem." [77]

The leader has a job to do. It is either given or created by him and people respect this activity. **"...the leaders of more effective groups tend to be those who are concerned with successful completion of the task if the situation is either very easy or very difficult for the leader. When the situation is of intermediate difficulty, the most effective leader is one who**

---

[77] *Interpersonal Diagnosis of Personality*, p. 15

devotes his attention primarily to friendly interpersonal relations." [78] Schiffer feels that Weber does not give enough importance to Group Psychology and that the social actors who follow Weber's charismatic leaders, within his texts, do so blindly.

Group dynamics suggests that direction is provided by the leader. Again there is an emphasis on interpersonal relations which implies that the method and delivery of communication is important. These are goal oriented people (at that point in time) that serve to deal with specific sets of problems or failing to recognize a problem situation will most likely serve to prop up a desk and appear as a symbolic figurehead. This probably more likely behavior in non-crises situations.

When defining 'leader' it is important to consider that, **"...any member of a group exerts leadership to the extent that the properties of the group are modified by his presence in the group...leadership and group performance are conceived as necessarily related to each other."** [79]

"He {the leader} must be aware that a given function is needed. He must feel that he is able to perform it, that he has enough skill to do so, or that it is safe for him to attempt to do so." [80]

---

[78] *Group Dynamics: Research and Theory*, Ed., Cartwright and Zander, Harper & Row, 1968 3rd edition, p. 302

[79] *Ibid*, p. 304
[80] Ibid, p. 310

This is the miracle worker. As long as she performs wonders she is in. As long as the goal lies ahead and appears possible the charismatic will be respected.

Again, basic concepts of group dynamics suggest that the charismatic is a protective type and will go to great lengths to provide for their needs. **"The social actor will respond to those who have not rejected him and if the group provides warmth and acceptance the actor will defend and even go on the offensive for them."**[81]

[81] Ibid, p. 310-311

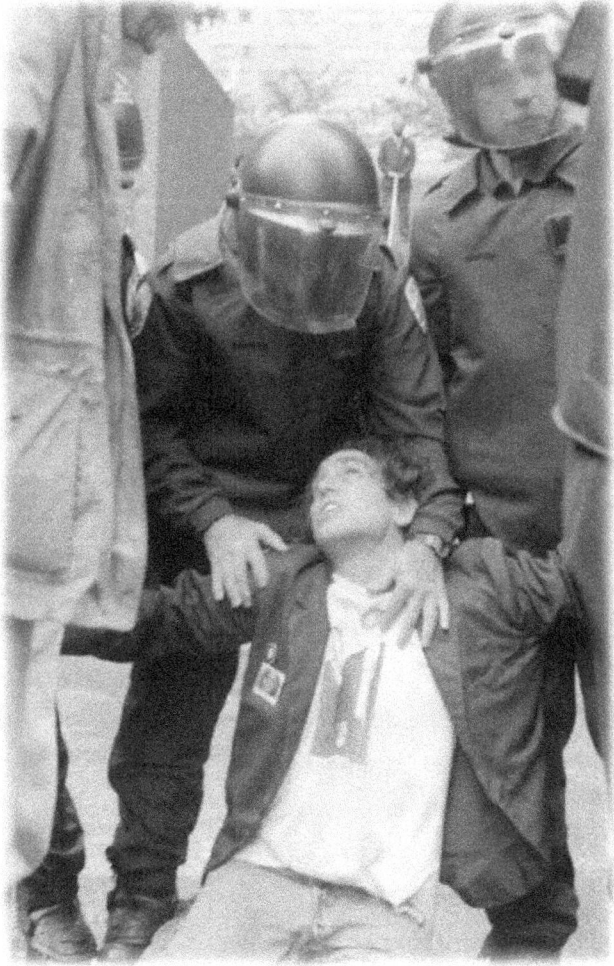

Berger – Thrills and Chills

The charismatic seeks change, drifts towards those who need change, and will provide what is necessary to bring about social action or possibly redirect existing social action by providing a more comfortable avenue or venue of escape from the crisis moment.

Charisma and Deviance

The charismatic leader – is he a tertiary deviant? The social actor has no choice when it comes to seeing the light. They are devoid of all other encumbrances.

Process of Becoming a Secondary Deviant or Lemart's Identity Stabilizing Model of Deviance [82]

1. **Primary deviation.**
2. **Social penalties.**
3. **Further primary deviation.**
4. **Stronger penalties and rejection of and against deviant.**
5. **Further deviation. Hostility and resentment may be focused on the punishers.**
6. **Community formally stigmatizes deviant as society tolerance is breached.**
7. **Deviant conduct reacts to stigma and penalties by reinforcing behavior.**
8. **Ultimate acceptance of deviant social status based on associated role.**

---

[82] *Deviant Behavior*, Alex Thio, p. 57

Kitsue goes on to call those who reject deviant status 'tertiary deviants'. [83] Because of their resolve and strength to reject external controls, the tertiary norm violator and the charismatic leader may be followed. Their moments of force and delivery in a community may be a pivotal point in the stream of that community's laws, customs, and mores.

Both Kitsue and Lemart's definition of the deviant do indeed closely match that of Weber's charismatic whose, **"...boundaries are established by someone drawing his legitimacy only from sources within himself."** [84]

This is a pretty key concept that our phantom charismatic could be so bold as to cry from the hill top that, *"You are all wrong to hold onto your beliefs and that only I am right and care no longer for the negative reactions of others."*

If we accept that there is a mutual relationship between the charismatic and the potential follower then each is deviating from the norm. Each is involved in a process of creating something new and different from what existed in the past. **"...a significant psychological factor in leadership – namely that all leaders, including the charismatic, are to a meaningful degree creations of the people."** [85] To oversimplify,

---

[83] Ibid, p. 59

[84] *Charisma*, Schiffer, p.4

[85] *Charisma, a psychoanalytic look at mass society*, Schiffer, University of Toronto Press, 1973, p. 6

the old order breaks down, there is a period of confusion, new orders are examined, then whatever is routinized is the accepted new order. This is not to suggest that is a 1-2-3 process. There may be a struggle back and forth along this continuum at any point, for a varying length of time, until the least exhausted social actor or order assumes priority.

The leader, the rebel, the social actor who stands out is deviating from the norm. Calvin is the deviator. Calvinists are conforming to Calvin but not conforming to the previous order. Calvin would have got nowhere if he had stood before the crowd and admitted that although he was wrong they should follow him anyway. The charismatic recognizes the hardship of being right, in so much as we all think subjectively. This is the value rational logic at work. The deviant who feels he is wrong is certainly different from the deviant who thinks he is right.

The possible outcome of the tertiary deviant, if he is powerful enough, will be to walk in the political field.

There are many more who are designated followers than leaders. In times of crises or panic the first person to shout, *"This way out!"*, in a theatre fire *or "Off the Pigs!"*, in a riot may be followed. But a lasting following, this is a following that will continue until the goal is reached must be inspired by one who the potential followers believe will save their skins. People naturally want to be on the winning side of an event, a war, a love affair or political ideology. It is better to live than to die, to feel good rather than feel pain. Karen Horney has pointed out that indeed it may be better to feel less pain than a lot. The lesser anxiety may be chosen.

I believe that it is for these reasons that fascism will always rise above pacifism. One can not fight back with peace and expect the pacifist to win, it would be oxymoronic. It is not a struggle unless there is contention, unless there is coercion coming from all participants,. because there is less anxiety to survive than there is to survive the blows.

The people have to have a want and desire to view greatness, to thrust greatness upon the candidate. There must be a need, real or imaginary, for anyone to elect a charismatic leader. The masses must be empowered with a motive. The human average 'ideal type' I believe is someone who will do things reluctantly and only if he has to. If there is a reason to not act he will take it. That was a paraphrase of Sutherland's rule number six.

This brings me to a small typography which illustrates movement towards the election of a leader.

Anxiety > Durkheim's Anomie >

Anxiety Avoidance > Charismatic Leader

Emile Durkheim speaks of social needs throughout much of his work. As much as I think that society occasionally needs revolution, I also wonder when society needs to be lulled into complacency and acquiescence. Need and motivation then may be quite similar. If we examine the roots of motivation, we will come up with the sources of information available to society's members.

The bias of the information, the space provided for dissenting views, and the level at which the masses may participate in this intellectual exchange may, to an extent, provide the direction for motivation or as Weber has so aptly summed up in his texts, *'Social action requires ideas, belief and direction.'*

People of conscience, men like Martin Luther who 'could do no other', women like Ellen Gabriel who spoke plain words, are not people of bravery or courage. They act on the sum total of all they have learned and do so without choice. They can not run. They can not hide. There is nothing for them to do but speak and act.

The role of an ideal charismatic leader may be comparable to that of a marriage counselor in that each tries to work herself out of a job and routinize the ideals they struggled for. The popular leader who rises to the top does so in confrontation with the leaders who have risen by means of traditional election, contest, or birth.

Conclusion

I believe that the unrest in Eastern Europe, Korea, China and the impact of the Gulf War itself have begun to spread their influence to North America. The empowerment is the idea that the individual is of greater value than the bureaucracy which monitors him or her.

Here in Canada a series of events, which I will arbitrarily say began with Oka, Quebec on July 11, 1990, have unfolded to encompass a growing segment of society. In less than a nine-month period Canadians have had to face an unpopular war overseas, an economic downturn, and a body of aboriginals which have shown the will to confront the state with armed resistance.

The world has not grown less complicated and extreme actions on behalf of governments and institutions around the world have revealed their brutalities. Few issues are black and white but fear and severe want can empower the masses to move. They do so reluctantly and only if they have to. They must have little or nothing to lose, nowhere else to go, and nowhere to hide like, the charismatic.

Here lies the fuel for the charismatic, should they be racist, egalitarian, humanist or capitalist. In times of anomic crises, the vacuum of normlessness and double messages can be filled by anyone who is seen as having answers and actions that will diminish the state of anxiety. Malcom X, Gandhi, Martin Luther King, Adolph Hitler, Mother Teresa and Timothy Leary were all people who were seen to have answers in their time within their context. Until they were defeated by death, disgrace, or failure each had a significant following. The book remains to be closed on any one of them. The impact of their lives remains with us today. Pacifists, fighters, and lovers may all find room for their message if the time is right. The timing seems to be the ability to speak when people want to listen.

The charismatic must contend with many ideas and implications of enormous complexity and do so often within seconds or days. They have to be themselves as this is the only way to make split-second judgements that are consistent and regular. Their minds are clear on one point, that they have no choice but to speak out as individuals' bar nothing.

I believe revolution comes only when it has to. Civil war only when the people have been divided by that which has been threatened by the charismatic leader. Witness Yugoslavia which had a popular leader uniting the masses in revolution in March of 1991, and when the Government threw him in jail all that was left was civil war because of a divided people with no one to believe in except the domination of fear and military coercion.

If moderates and reformers are seen to do their job the charismatic need not to do his as there is no anxiousness, vacuum or need to fill. Otherwise to stand by and watch with the power of passive acquiescence is irresponsible.

Perhaps a final clue to what charisma is composed of is to be found in Emile Durkheim's comments on the impact of sociology in his tract, *"On the Principles of 1789 and Sociology"*. When one separates the principles of revolution from the context of time, place, and spirit. He was talking about the components of individuality.

"They start from the abstract concept of the individual in himself and from it develop the contents. Given the notion of an absolutely autonomous individual, depending only on himself, without historical antecedents, without social milieu, how should

he conduct himself either in his economic relations or in his moral life?" [86]

In fact at this stage in the charismatic's life he/she is very much alone, trusting only their own speculations, guided by the sum total of all their knowledge and experience. Here the charismatic is influenced only by the environment that directly effects their senses of taste, touch, sight, sound, and smell. They believe only what they actually observe with their own senses of critical understanding to be real. In a near solipsistic way, the charismatic may decide that a news event reported in the media was only actual if they personally observed it. Nothing is truly believed except that which has been experienced first-hand. I believe this separation of the self from the environment is one of the most important principles that guides the charismatic's action.

Perhaps if the charismatic comes into contact at about this point with others who are sharing a similar willing suspension of disbelief in a crisis situation a following may develop. Then both the charismatic and the following may empower one another exponentially.

When Durkheim wrote, *The Intellectual Elite and Democracy* he was advising scholars of the time and place to "leave their laboratories and libraries to draw nearer the masses."

---

[86] *On Morality and Society*, Emile Durkheim, University of Chicago Press, 1973, p. 37

These ideas, beliefs and direction for intellectuals of course fall very much into line with Weber's own thoughts on the principles of social action. Durkheim's bias is certainly more upfront, obvious, and simplistic than Weber's. His bite size tracts remind me of broadsheets tacked up in public places simple enough for the unschooled citizen to comprehend. I believe that Durkheim was more interested in empowering the masses and placing the right of the individual above those of the state in contrast to the difficulties Weber felt people might have, understanding means and values foreign to their own ideology. A difficulty he felt that might be encountered by those **"...who abhor extreme rationalist fanaticism (such as the fanatic advocacy of the rights of man)."** [87] Weber correctly identified the rational economic system as mechanistic, depersonalizing, and offensive routine. [88] I don't feel I've be venturing far from base if I said that mechanistic, depersonalizing, and offensive routine may produce anxiety, a state of behavior and emotion that may be dynamic background for the process of charisma to develop.

Emile Durkheim would most certainly have aided Timothy Leary in his bid to resist the physical coercion of a para-military attack on a self-determined nation. Max Weber might have seen a man, with a calling, elected to

---

[87] *Economy and society*, p. 6
[88] *From Max Weber*, p. 50

High Priest status and Max may have stood on the sidelines, along with the F.B.I., recording all the details. Weber knew that physical coercion would certainly win against an un-united front of psychedelic self-healers on a mystical trip to the inner eye. Durkheim, in contrast, would have had no choice but to join the crowd of believers and egg on the masses to greater esprit, using his powers to aid the revolution.

Bibliography

Thomas Kuhn, The Structure of Scientific Revolution

J.E.T. Eldridge, ed. *Max Weber: The Interpretation of Social Reality*. London, Joseph, 1970

Max Weber. Economy and Society: An Outline of Interpretive Sociology. Ed. Guenther Roth & Claus Wittich (New York, Bedminster Press, 1968)

Report of the Special Joint Committee on a Renewed Canada (Ottawa: Supply and Services, 1992).

Government of Canada, *Shaping Canada's Future Together: Proposals* (Ottawa: Supply and Services, 1991).

Max Weber on Universities. Ed & trans. Edward Shils, Chicago, University of Chicago Press, 1974

H.H. Gerth & C. Mills, eds & trans. From Max Weber (London, Routledge & Kegan Paul 1970

Julian Assange, Sun 31 Dec 2006: *The non-linear effects of leaks on unjust systems of governance*. Web archive.

Starhawk. *Truth or Dare: Encounters With Power, Authority, and Mastery,* San Francisco, Harper & Row, 1990

The London Chronicle, July 5-7, 1791

The Montreal Mirror, March 26, 1992

Erika Mann. *School for Barbarians: Education Under the Nazis* (London, Lindsay Drummond Ltd., 1939)

See *Kanehsatake 270 Years of Resistance*, Alanis Obomsawin, National Film Board, 1993

Lewis H. Gann. *Guerrillas in History*, Hoover Institution Press, Stanford University, 3rd print, 1975

Gerard Chaliand, *Terrorism: From Popular Struggle to Media Spectacle* London: Atlantic Highlands, N.J. Saqi Boos, 1987

Albert Memmi. *Dominated Men: Notes Towards a Portrait*, Boston, Beacon Press, 1968

Frederique Apffel Marglin & Stephen A. Marglin. *Dominating Knowledge* Oxford, Clarendon Press; New York, Oxford University Press, 1990

Frederic Lilge. *The Abuse of Learning: The Failure of the German University*, New York, Macmillan Co., 1948

The Essential Rousseau, trans. Lowell Bair, Meridian, 1983

The City and Man, Leo Strauss, Chicago, Rand McNally & Company, 1964
Economy and Society, University of California Press, Max Weber, ed. Roth & Wittich,

The Scientist's Role In Society, Ben David, Chicago, 1984

Interpersonal Diagnosis of Personality: A Functional theory and Methodology for Personality Evaluation, Timothy Leary, Ronald Press, 1957

The Montreal Gazette, May 18, 1991

The Link, Concordia University, March 20th, 1992

Press For Conversion, Issue 3, 1990

Revolution for the Hell of It, by Free, Dial Press, 10th print, 1970

Deviant Behavior, Alex Thio, 3rd edition, Harper & Row, 1990

I'm Your Man, Leonard Cohen, 1987

Group Dynamics: Research and Theory, Ed., Cartwright and Zander, Harper & Row, 1968 3rd edition

Charisma, a psychoanalytic look at mass society, Schiffer, University of Toronto Press, 1973

On Morality and Society, Emile Durkheim, University of Chicago Press, 1973

Everywhere They Are In Chains: Political Theory from Rousseau to Marx,, University of Toronto , Nelson, 1988, Horowitz & Horowitz

Modern Political Theory from Hobbes to Marx – Key Debates, ed. By J. Livly & A. Reeve, Routledge, 1989

www.ingramcontent.com/pod-product-compliance
Lightning Source LLC
Chambersburg PA
CBHW022117280326
41933CB00007B/431